the Noodle bowl

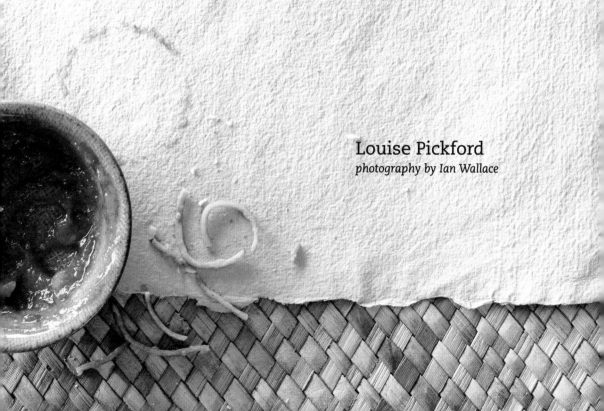

the Noodle bowl

Over 70 recipes for Asian-inspired noodle dishes

Louise Pickford

photography by Ian Wallace

Senior Designer Sonya Nathoo
Commissioning Editor Stephanie Milner
Production Controller Mai-ling Collyer
Art Director Leslie Harrington
Editorial Director Julia Charles
Publisher Cindy Richards

Food Stylist Louise Pickford
Prop Stylist Tony Hutchinson
Indexer Vanessa Bird

First published in 2015
This revised edition published in 2020
by Ryland Peters & Small
20–21 Jockey's Fields
London WC1R 4BW
and
341 East 116th Street
New York NY 10029
www.rylandpeters.com

Text © Louise Pickford 2015, 2020
Design and photographs © Ryland Peters
& Small 2015, 2020

ISBN: 978-1-78879-235-6

10 9 8 7 6 5 4 3 2 1

Printed and bound in China.

CIP data from the Library of Congress has been
applied for. A CIP record for this book is available
from the British Library.

Notes
• Both British (metric) and American (imperial
plus US cups) are included in these recipes for
your convenience; however it is important to work
with one set of measurements and not alternate
between the two within a recipe.
• All spoon measurements are level unless
otherwise specified.
• All eggs are medium (UK) or large (US),
unless specified as large, in which case US extra
large should be used. Uncooked or partially
cooked eggs should not be served to the very old,
frail, young children, pregnant women or those
with compromised immune systems.
• Ovens should be preheated to the specified
temperatures. We recommend using an oven
thermometer. If using a fan-assisted oven, adjust
temperatures according to the manufacturer's
instructions.
• When a recipe calls for the grated zest of citrus
fruit, buy unwaxed fruit and wash well before using.
If you can only find treated fruit, scrub well in
warm soapy water before using.
• To sterilize preserving jars, wash them in hot,
soapy water and rinse in boiling water. Place in
a large saucepan and cover with hot water. With
the saucepan lid on, bring the water to a boil and
continue boiling for 15 minutes. Turn off the heat
and leave the jars in the hot water until just
before they are to be filled. Invert the jars onto
a clean dish towel to dry. Sterilize the lids for
5 minutes, by boiling or according to the
manufacturer's instructions. Jars should be filled
and sealed while they are still hot.

Korean chilled noodles with egg

'Balachung' – delicious deep-fried crispy shallots from Myanmar

Contents

Delicious fresh egg noodles served hot, straight from the wok

Asian noodles in all their glorious forms

This book celebrates what I feel is best about noodles, noodle dishes and their origins. It doesn't claim to be a noodle bible, more a close look at the variety and versatility of this wonderful food. I have a passion for everything noodle and I hope I can share my enthusiasm with the following collection of recipes.

Although I had travelled to Asia and the Far East before, it was my move to Sydney in 2000 that introduced me to a far wider range of cuisines from those countries. Australia with its multicultural society is home to a large population of Asian immigrants including Chinese, Japanese, Thai, Vietnamese, Cambodian, Laotian, Korean, Indonesian and more besides. You don't have to travel far in Sydney to find an ethnic restaurant and even in our local suburb we had two Thai restaurants, a Japanese, a Chinese, a Vietnamese café, two Indonesian restaurants and a South-east Asian noodle bar.

Living in that region for 13 years enabled me to experience a whole gambit of new and exciting dishes. Not only did I discover foods with flavours that literally explode in your mouth (not just the chillies/chiles), I found a lighter, healthier and more balanced diet: fresh vibrant salads, pungent aromatic broths packed with crisp raw vegetables and fragrant herbs; stir-fried vegetables and meat dishes, where meat is used sparingly and is only a tiny part of the whole meal.

It was however noodles that really captured my imagination. I was hooked from the first time I went to a small Japanese noodle bar in central Sydney where you could watch the fresh noodles being made daily

and then get to eat them moments later in a variety of simple yet divine dishes. The texture was something else – so silky and succulent with a slight chewiness in a delicately flavoured broth. It was the beginning of my love affair with this simple food.

I cook a lot, I cook for work, I share my love of food with my husband, friends and family and I hope I have put together a balanced recipe book with delicious noodle dishes from across Asia.

A LITTLE HISTORY

Noodles are centuries old and there has been much contention over where noodles first originated. If you include Italy, as well as other noodle-producing countries outside Asia, the dispute has been raging almost as long as the noodle itself. However, it is now accepted that noodles were first introduced in the Han Province in China, around 200 AD.

Certainly in both China and Japan, noodles have a huge cultural significance. In China, the noodle symbolizes longevity; it is served at birthday celebrations, and cutting a noodle into lengths is considered to bring bad luck. In Japan it represents the beginning of the New Year and the rising of the moon.

For centuries noodles have been prepared by hand and eaten either fresh or hung out in the sun to dry. Today, most noodles we buy in the West are made by machine and sold pre-cooked to be rehydrated, although you can buy fresh noodles from Asian food stores. Throughout Asia noodles are still mostly prepared and sold fresh. Family-run noodle shops are everywhere and the art of noodle-making is passed on through the generations.

We all have to eat, of course, but whenever I have been to Asian countries I have been blown away by just how important food is to the culture of the people. Food sustains but also it is embedded in people's religious beliefs, their sense of family and the community. Holy days are numerous and a huge part of these celebrations is focused on food gifts as a form of thanksgiving. These do exist in the West of course, but I don't think to quite the same extent.

There is little doubt that Asia, from north to south, is a melting pot of cultures, traditions, religions and peoples but most of all it is a rich source of some of our most exciting and interesting food dishes.

THE PRACTICALITIES
I remember early trips to Asian supermarkets and the overwhelming quantity of row after row of different shapes, sizes and colours of noodles. It can be a little daunting, especially if you are new to Asian cooking, so I want this book to help guide you and help you understand what type of noodle is best for each recipe.

I have made every effort to ensure that the ingredients, while as authentic as possible, are obtainable. If I have included an ingredient that is hard to find locally, I offer an alternative. The ingredient identification pages at the beginning of the book will help you to recognize some of the more unusual ingredients, whilst a comprehensive glossary at the back (see pages 156–157) will provide information on the rest.

One question I get asked a lot is should one use fresh or dried noodles? I tend to use fresh noodles (when I can get them) in the more delicate dishes like salads or soups and then dried in stir-fries, but they are pretty interchangeable. I give a specific noodle type in each recipe but you can vary this if you like or are unable to find a certain type.

Of the noodle varieties included in this book, fresh noodles (in the West these are usually wheat noodles) need a short cooking time. They are plunged into a large saucepan of boiling water and once they have returned to the boil are cooked for 2–3 minutes depending on the their width. Dried wheat noodles also need to be cooked, but for longer, at least 4 minutes but no more than 5 minutes. Rice noodles, cellophane noodles and sweet potato noodles only need soaking before they are used in a recipe. Times are given in each recipe, but to expand slightly on this, I have experimented with differing soaking and cooking times when testing the recipes and not all were conclusive. Consequently, I recommend using my cooking and soaking times as a guide and testing different noodle brands as you go.

If a noodle is being rehydrated to be eaten without any secondary form of cooking, in a salad or soup they will perhaps require a little longer than if they are to be cooked twice, in a stir-fry for example.

Noodles in themselves, have very little flavour but it is this that makes them so versatile. Noodles absorb the flavours around them and help to balance and soften some of the more fiery and punchy ingredients in Asian cooking. However, it isn't just about taste – noodles are all about texture. Think soft, chewy, slurpy, nutty, crunchy, crispy and you'll have an idea of just how many wonderful textures you will explore with the recipes in this book.

And finally, because the culture of the countries in which these recipe are based celebrate food as part of the sharing process with family and friends, I am hoping that you will be able to share some of my favourite noodles dishes, as I do with mine.

noodle basics

Noodle know-how

Sometimes it's the little things in life that are most rewarding, and in a funny kind of a way I feel that the recipes in this first chapter are that for me. A good example is the recipe for Chicken stock (see page 25). I doubt that when you first look through the following pages you will stop at this page and go, 'Wow, I simply MUST cook this now!' But when you make the stock and use it in one of the recipes further along, you will get it. It is simply not possible for the resulting dish to be a winner if the stock is not good. Yes of course you can go and buy a stock/bouillon cube, or one of the new little stock 'jellies', or even a liquid stock, but the stock in this book is designed to work for the recipes in which it is to be used. It packs a big hit of garlic and ginger, has a real depth of flavour imbibed by the cooking time and I believe the fact that the chicken is cut up before being simmered adds a further flavour dimension. And this is what I mean. Get the basics right and the rest will reward you time and time again.

Have a look through this chapter and get a feel for what lies ahead. We have fragrant flavoured Chilli and Garlic oils (see page 22), aromatic pastes and fiery sauces, Deep-fried shallots (see page 29) and other crispy condiments that will transform a simple broth into an unforgettable one. Hot salsa, cool dipping sauces and the funkiest salt and pepper condiment ever in Yin yang lime juice (see page 26).

Food is also served and eaten differently in Asia. I like to think of it more like grazing – smaller dishes served frequently throughout the day. No single main dish, rather lots of little dishes with accompaniments. You have rice and noodles providing the starch content while meat or fish play a small part and the protein is often provided by tofu in its many guises. These dishes are then surrounded by lots of fresh, mainly raw dishes of sliced vegetables, fresh herbs, chillies/chiles, sauces and dips for extra flavour, and crispy titbits for texture. It's sociable, it's noisy and it's delicious.

If you have ever eaten in a Chinese restaurant you will notice instead of salt and pepper on the table there is always dark soy sauce, chilli/chile oil and chilli/chile sauce, all to add a little more depth to a dish. Dumplings come bathed in piquant sauces like the Szechuan chilli dressing (see page 33) or something needing a more delicate touch like the Chinese dipping sauce (see page 26).

Japanese accompaniments are subtler; dipping sauces are less hot, Dashi broth (see page 25) is clear and fat-free with a cleaner taste. Pickles are very popular and are served as palette cleansers or as a garnish, like the Pickled cucumber (see page 30). In summer, soba noodles are traditionally served cold with a bowl of simple Dipping sauce (see page 26), while big bowls of steaming noodle soups are fabulous for chilly winter days.

Sharing a border with China to the north and the islands of Japan to the east, strong influences of the two can be found in Korean cooking. Like their close neighbours the Koreans are lovers of the noodle – mainly wheat and buckwheat. However Korea does produce a different noodle made from sweet potato starch known as 'japchae' (see page 15). Translucent and pale brown in colour, japchae have a wonderfully glutinous texture with a slight bite to them. Korean food tends to be fiery hot and their chilli/chile powder gochugaru is an example of this. It is used in making kimchi (see page 30), Korea's national dish, which is served as a condiment at every meal. Their dips (see page 34) too are traditionally hot so I have moderated the quantity of chilli/chile to those recipes to suit a more temperate palette, but if you like your food with a kick, simply increase the amount.

As you travel further into South-east Asia the landscape and agriculture changes and although northern regions of Vietnam, Laos and Thailand produce wheat noodles we now start to see a predominance of rice noodles the further south you go. These countries, along with Myanmar, also share many significant similarities in their dishes. Many more salads are eaten; fresh vegetables, often served raw, are tossed with hot, sharp, salty and sweet sauces. There are salsa-like sauces such as Vietnamese Nuoc cham and Thai Green nam jim (both page 37), and fish sauce takes over from soy sauce to add saltiness to the dishes.

Even further south we have Malaysia and Singapore, where we see the return of the culinary influences of China with a large Chinese migrant population and the ancient trading routes that developed strong links with these countries. This in turn gives us a wide mixture of flavours and ingredients depending on the regions but both rice and wheat noodles are used. Coconut milk from Thai cooking is used extensively and to the west lies India and with a large Indian population in both countries we see a greater use of spices such as turmeric. The chilli/chile sauces, or Sambal olek (see page 38) as they are known, include fresh turmeric, adding another twist to this well-travelled sauce.

So take a little time and stock up on core ingredients – you will find that the recipes ahead will reward you for your efforts and many of the basics, once made, keep well either in a screw-top jar on the shelf or in a plastic container in the fridge. The stocks can be made ahead and frozen.

Oodles of noodles

Noodles along with rice are at the very heart of Asian cooking, providing the building blocks to what is a varied, healthy and fascinating cuisine. Noodles are mostly served as one-pot dishes in soups, salads and stir-fries. They provide the carbohydrate element alongside fresh vegetables, herbs, meat and fish, balancing the nutritional benefits of each dish. In order to make sense of the staggering variety of noodles in our stores I have divided them according to the type of starch used to make them.

In general terms, all South-east Asian countries use some or all of the noodle varieties featured here but independently favour one type over others, mainly due to what grows well in a particular region. Within each variety we find a huge range of shapes and sizes of noodle, some with very specific uses. Along with this, the preparation changes from one type to another; some dried noodles need to be pre-cooked before being added to a dish, while others simply need to be pre-soaked. Fresh noodles need to be cooked, but only for a minute or two. Details of exact soaking or cooking times can be found in individual recipes rather than by noodle type.

Noodles are more readily available in their dried form in the West, but you will find fresh noodles in Asian food stores. Fresh noodles must be stored in the fridge but should be eaten within 2–3 days of purchase. Dried noodles will keep indefinitely, sealed in a plastic bag in the store cupboard.

Wheat flour noodles

As the name implies, these are made with wheat flour and water (or sometimes flour and oil) and are the oldest variety of noodle. They are flat, thin or medium-fat as well as made into sheets for wrappers. The finer noodles are used in delicate soups while thicker varieties appear in hearty stews and stir-fries. They are off-white or grey-white in colour. Both fresh and dried noodles need to be pre-cooked before use. As a rule, boil fresh noodles for 1–2 minutes and dried noodles for 4–5 minutes, both until al dente. Wheat flour noodles have a chewy texture and a slightly savoury flavour.

SOMEN
Japanese noodles are enriched with oil, resulting in a thin and delicate noodle that comes wrapped in bunches. Used in a similar way to soba noodles, they are more refined and slightly more delicate.

UDON
A fat Japanese noodle with a slippery, chewy texture. Ideally suited to soups, it must be slurped through the teeth, allowing the noodle to cool slightly as it goes down. Dried udon noodles can be round or flat and are a creamy white colour.

SOBA
Made with a combination of wheat and buckwheat flour, soba noodles are light to dark brown in colour with a rich nutty flavour and slight bite. They can be flavoured with other ingredients such as green tea powder and are commonly served cold in dishes throughout Japan.

RAMEN
Ramen is both the name of a Japanese dish as well as a type of noodle and is more commonly associated with instant noodles. Ramen noodles can be white or yellow

Fresh wheat noodles

Fresh egg noodles

Green tea
soba noodles

Buckwheat soba noodles

as some are made with egg and are formed into tight, twisted clusters. They are mainly used in soups.

GYOZA WRAPPERS

Small rounds of wheat flour dough are used to make delicate Japanese dumplings. They are sold fresh or frozen in packs and need no pre-cooking or soaking.

EGG NOODLES

Often referred to as 'Chinese egg noodles', these are made with flour and eggs, the dried noodles come either as sticks or in clusters and are pale yellow in colour. Fresh egg noodles are available from Asian food stores and are usually formed into coils. You can also buy vacuum-packed noodles, which should be rinsed under boiling water before use. Egg noodles have a texture most like pasta but tend to be slightly chewier.

EGG THREAD NOODLES

The thinnest of noodles, these are also called 'yakisoba noodles' and are mostly packaged as nests or clusters and are always sold dried.

FLAT CHINESE NOODLES

Similar to linguine, these are usually sold fresh in the chilled section of supermarkets.

HOKKEIN NOODLES

Chinese in origin, Hokkein noodles are hugely popular in Malaysia. They are reasonably fat and similar to spaghetti. Fresh Hokkein noodles should be rinsed before pre-cooking and tossed in oil to prevent sticking.

WONTON WRAPPERS

Small squares or rounds of fresh egg noodle dough used to make Chinese dumplings. They are sold either chilled or frozen and come in packs of up to 40 sheets. They need no soaking or pre-cooking before use.

SPRING ROLL WRAPPERS

For Chinese-style spring rolls, these wrappers are also made with flour and water. However, they are far thinner than wonton wrappers and traditionally sold square. They are readily available in Asian stores, usually frozen, and don't need to be soaked or pre-cooked.

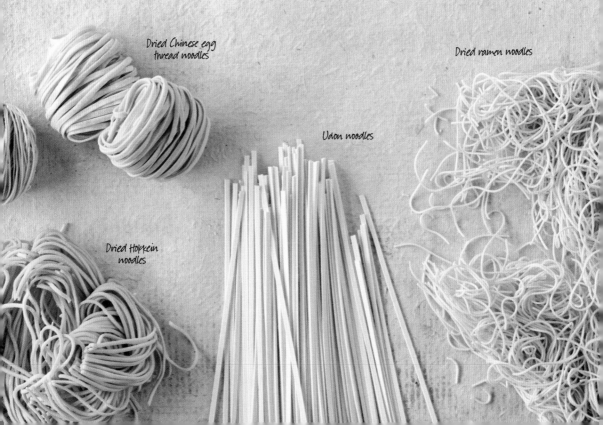

Dried Chinese egg thread noodles

Dried ramen noodles

Udon noodles

Dried Hokkein noodles

Rice and other noodles

Made from extracted rice flour paste, rice noodles are virtually tasteless. They come in all different shapes, from the very fine rice vermicelli noodles to rice sticks, flat rice noodles and rice noodle sheets, wraps and papers. They are used in stir-fries, soups, salads and snacks. Rice noodles only need to be soaked before being used. This varies from 5–20 minutes depending on the type of noodle and how thick it is. Rice noodles have a more slippery texture than wheat, and although fresh rice noodles are available from Asian stores they are more readily available dried. Fresh noodles are bright white, while dried rice noodles are a dull white or off-white colour until soaked, when they turn white.

RICE VERMICELLI

Tiny, very thin noodles sold dried in tightly packed strips, these light, delicate noodles are commonly used in salads and clear soups and should have a slight bite.

RICE STICK NOODLES

Probably best known as the pad Thai noodle, they are about 3 mm/$\frac{1}{8}$ in. wide. Once soaked, they turn from a dull grey or white to bright white. They should be soft but still retain a little bite and have a slippery texture.

RICE PAPER WRAPPERS

Although not strictly a noodle, these wafer-thin dried wrappers or skins are made with the same dough as noodles. Normally sold dried in rounds, they also come in squares or triangles. They need dipping in warm water for about 30–60 seconds until softened. They are used to make fresh rice wrapper rolls.

BLACK RICE NOODLES

A fairly new addition to our stores, these are made using black rice and some colouring. They look similar to Japanese noodles and come in small bundles. They are available from some specialist food stores or online.

CELLOPHANE NOODLES

Also called 'bean thread', 'mung bean' or 'glass' noodles, these opaque threads are made from mung beans (or sometimes tapioca starch). Although largely

Dried rice stick noodles

Korean sweet potato noodles

tasteless it is the texture that makes these noodles so intriguing. They are glutinous and slippery and great for soaking up the flavour of whatever sauce they are combined with. Like rice noodles, cellophane noodles only need pre-soaking for anything from 3–5 minutes and always in boiling water. The dried noodle is very white, but as soon as they are soaked they tend to become transparent, hence the nickname 'glass noodles'.

SWEET POTATO NOODLES

Similar to cellophane noodles, sweet potato noodles (or 'japchae') are a staple of Korean food. They are a medium thick, long glass noodle with a rather unappetizing grey-brown colour, both dried and cooked. They have a rather wonderful chewy, slippery texture and mild earthy flavour. They need to be pre-cooked before use in boiling water for 2–3 minutes, until al dente.

Rice paper wrappers

Dried rice vermicelli noodles

Dried flat rice noodles

Dried cellophane noodles or 'glass noodles' or 'mung bean noodles'

Fresh produce

It's important to shop well and choose the freshest produce you can find and then to store it well.

SNAKE BEANS

Also known as 'Chinese' or 'yard-long' beans, these green pods grow up to 40 cm/16 in. in length, hence their name. Native to the warmer regions of South- and Far East Asia they are used in salads, soups and stir-fries and can be eaten fresh or cooked. Green beans can be substituted if you can't find snake beans.

GREEN PAPAYA

Papaya trees grow really well in the warm climate of Vietnam and its neighbouring countries and papaya fruit is valued as both a fruit and a vegetable. Shredded young papaya is added to salads or pickled in Vietnam.

ASIAN SHALLOTS

Smaller than other onion varieties, Asian shallots are tiny reddish-purple garlic clove-sized bulbs. The flavour is milder than European varieties. Shallots (and garlic) are best stored in a dark place out of the fridge.

PAK CHOI/BOK CHOY

A type of Chinese cabbage, this crispy, crunchy green vegetable is often braised with oyster sauce and is delicious in both soups and salads, raw or cooked.

Keep this and all other greens in zip lock bags in the fridge.

PUFFED TOFU

Found in the chilled section in Asian supermarkets, puffed tofu is made from deep-fried squares of bean curd. They are light and spongy with an almost hollow centre that allows them to absorb liquids, so are ideal for adding to soups and stews. Once opened they should be kept chilled and used within three days. Unlike other types of tofu, puffed tofu freezes well.

PEA SHOOTS AND TENDRILS

These add both add flavour and texture to salads and can be used as a garnish for soups and stir-fries. Pea shoots tend to be readily available in the vegetable section of supermarkets, while tendrils are more specialized and seasonal. Try online suppliers.

FRESH CHILLIES/CHILES Perhaps the most important ingredient in South-east Asian cooking, chillies/chiles come in all shapes, sizes and heat. If you prefer a milder dish, remove the seeds – the smaller the chilli/chile, the hotter. Chillies/chiles keep well chilled in an airtight container or zip-lock bag.

CHOI SUM Sometimes called 'Chinese broccoli', this green stalked vegetable of the mustard family looks a little like a longer, thinner variety of pak choi/bok choy. The young shoots can be eaten raw in salads while the older stems are added to stir-fries.

ASIAN MUSHROOMS

A variety of mushrooms are used in Asian cooking including shiitake, oyster, shiro-shimeji and enoki and they are often sold in mixed packets. Mushrooms keep much better in either a paper or cloth bag.

Snake beans

Green papaya

Pea shoots

Chillies/chiles

Puffed tofu

Choi sum

Pak choi / bok choy

Asian shallots

Asian mushrooms

Herbs and spices

Where would we be without the wonderful array of exotic flavours from herbs and spices? Add a little Chinese five-spice powder or star anise to a chicken broth and immediately it tastes Asian. Likewise with Thai basil or lime leaves added to a salad. Leaf herbs, unlike spices, won't last long, but to keep them as fresh as possible, for as long as possible, trim the stalks and put in an airtight plastic container with a sprinkling of cold water. Store in the fridge and they should keep for up to a week. Spices last far longer but need to be sealed in an airtight container or screw-top jar. Roots and rhizomes can be sealed in a zip-lock bag and kept in the fridge.

GARLIC CHIVES

Like regular chives, these are members of the onion family but have a garlicky flavour. They are used extensively in Chinese cooking for a wonderful aromatic taste and are often called 'Chinese chives'. Visually they resemble a large, flat chive and are about twice as long. They are often added to salads and stir-fries.

THAI BASIL

A member of the basil family, of which there are numerous varieties, Thai basil, as the name implies, is grown widely in Thailand as well its neighbouring countries. It adds a wonderfully aromatic, aniseed flavour to soups, salads and stir-fries.

PERILLA LEAVES

Native to the mountainous regions of Asia, perilla is a member of the mint family, but is sometimes referred to as 'sesame leaves' (though unrelated). Widely used in Korean dishes, they are used throughout South-east Asia in salads. They appear similar to nettle leaves, are slightly furry with green-purple leaves and are favoured for their aromatic mint, basil and aniseed flavour. Use a combination of mint and Thai basil as substitute.

Garlic chives

Thai basil

Star anise

Szechuan peppercorns

Turmeric

Perilla leaves

SZECHUAN PEPPERCORNS

Also called 'Sichuan peppercorns' or 'Chinese coriander/cilantro', the brown-red husks alone are used as the black seeds inside are gritty and unpalatable. They have a delightful aromatic lemony flavour and although not hot, they have an almost zinging sensation on the tongue. Often toasted before being lightly ground and added to all manner of dishes.

TURMERIC ROOT

A close relative of ginger, fresh turmeric has a lighter, more vibrant flavour than the ground spice. Similar in appearance to ginger, the rhizome should be peeled to reveal the deep yellow flesh, which is then grated or pounded. If using ground turmeric, you will need half the amount of fresh listed in the recipe.

STAR ANISE

This pretty star-shaped spice originates from China and Vietnam and was introduced to Europe in the 17th century. It is not related to anise, although it shares a similar flavour, but is actually the dried fruit of a small oriental tree. It is perhaps the most important spice used in Chinese cuisine. Chinese five-spice powder is a good alternative if you can't find whole star anise.

GOCHUGARU

The Korean name for chilli powder – 'gochu' meaning chilli/chile and 'garu' powder – gochugaru is made from dried chillies/chiles that are less finely pounded than other chilli powders and has a deep earthy-red colour. Used extensively in Korean dishes, it has a slight smokey, fruity, sweet note with a high-powered kick.

GARLIC CHIVE FLOWERS

Like all flowers from the allium family, garlic chive flowers are edible, and also add a decorative touch to a dish.

GALANGAL ROOT

Related to ginger, galangal is also a rhizome and looks very similar to ginger, but with a thinner paler skin, often tinged with a pink hue, while the flesh is almost white. There are hints of ginger, pepper and even lemon.

FRESH MINT

Vietnamese mint, which has a very earthy flavour, somewhere between mint and coriander/cilantro, is sadly quite hard to buy unless you are lucky enough to live close to an Asian store, but is very easy to grow. Common mint can be used instead.

LEMON GRASS

A tropical grass native to India and Sri Lanka, although today it is also widely grown in other countries including California. It has a subtle lemon flavour and it is only the innermost part of the stalk that is tender.

Lemon grass

Gochugaru

Garlic chive flowers

Mint

Galangal

Store cupboard

It's always a good idea to keep a well-stocked store cupboard for non-perishables, especially the more unusual ingredients that you might need less often, as long as they keep well. Pastes and sauces will keep chilled in the fridge but always check use-by dates where applicable. I tend to shop large and less often for this type of ingredient especially if I have had to go further afield to buy what I need. Below are those that I feel are important for the recipes in this book. Many you may not come across every day, but they can be found in larger supermarkets, Asian stores or online.

DRIED KOMBU

A variety of edible kelp that grows prolifically in the seas around Japan, Korea and China, it is most prized by the Japanese and is the integral ingredient in dashi.

DRIED WAKAME SEAWEED

Normally sold dried in European and American stores, this is rehydrated and used in soups as well as salads. The tiny dried strands swell on contact with liquid and deliver a silky texture and sweet, nutty flavour.

SHAOXING RICE WINE

Also known as 'Chinese rice wine', shaoxing is the standard spirit used in Chinese cooking. Made from glutinous brown rice and deep amber in colour it has an earthy, nutty flavour. Although you could use another brand of rice wine I recommend finding shaoxing for a more authentic flavour.

BLACK SESAME SEEDS

Perhaps the oldest condiment known to man, sesame seeds have always been highly valued for their oil. These tiny, oval seeds have a nutty flavour and light crunch and come in different colours: black, white, brown or red. Often associated with Middle Eastern cooking, sesame seeds are also highly valued in Asian cooking. They most likely originated in India, where they are strewn over salads, stir-fries and soups.

Dried kombu

Black sesame seeds

Tamarind paste

Tamarind

Dried wakame seaweed

Palm sugar

PALM SUGAR

Made from the sap of a certain palm tree that grows throughout Africa and Asia, once processed into syrup it is either sold or crystalized into discs or blocks. Slightly less sweet than other sugars, it has a delicate caramel flavour. It is also called 'jaggery' or even 'coconut sugar' depending on the country of origin and should be shaved or grated and measured in tablespoons.

TAMARIND

The pod-like fruit of the tamarind tree, which although indigenous to tropical Africa has long been cultivated in India and across South-east Asia, has a distinctive sweet lemon flavour, adding a subtle sharpness to savoury dishes. You can buy it whole in pods, as a block of hard pulp or as a concentrate. Dilute the concentrate three parts to one part water for tamarind paste or three parts to two parts water for tamarind water.

DRIED BONITO FLAKES

Also known as 'katsuobushi' in Japan, these are dried, smoked flakes of the bonito fish. They have an intense smokiness to them, which adds flavour to Japanese Dashi broth (see page 25). Dashi broth can be made without them (for a vegetarian option) but I like to use them for the extra flavour they add. Once opened, as long as the packet is sealed, they will last indefinitely.

SHRIMP PASTE

Much like fish sauce, shrimp paste is used to add flavour in Thai, Vietnamese, Cambodian, Burmese, Laotian, Indonesian, Malaysian and Singaporean dishes. It is available plain or with other flavours added such as tomato, which I prefer to use for its vibrant colour. Once opened it needs to be stored in the fridge and used within 1 month.

PEANUTS

Used as a condiment in many South-east Asian dishes – especially in Thai, Vietnamese, Laotian, Burmese and Cambodian dishes – peanuts add texture as well as flavour to salads, stir-fries and soups, and are integral to pad Thai. For an authentic flavour, buy whole peanuts and shell as required. You can also buy pre-roasted peanuts in their shells, which add even more flavour.

DRIED SHRIMP

Small prawns/shrimp are dried in the sun to concentrate their flavour and preserve them. If you have ever travelled in Asia you will have come across baskets of these little chaps drying in the sun. It is this flavour that defines the cooking of Thailand, Vietnam, Laos, Burma and Cambodia (where soy sauce does the same in China, Japan and Korea). They will keep indefinitely if stored in a sealed jar set in a cool, dark place.

Shrimp paste

Dried shrimp

Dried bonito flakes

Peanuts

Chilli oil Asia

Chilli/chile oil (opposite, left) is a great addition to any store cupboard. Once strained the oil will keep in the fridge for a month but be sure to return to room temperature before use.

30 g/6 whole dried
  chillies/chiles
250 ml/1 cup peanut oil
sterilized glass bottle with
  an airtight cap

Makes 250 ml/1 cup

Put the chillies/chiles in a bowl, cover with hot water and leave to soak for 30 minutes until slightly softened. Drain well and discard the water. Put the softened chillies/chiles in a food processor and blend to a rough paste.

Transfer the paste to a small saucepan, pour in the oil and set over a medium heat to warm gently, until the mixtures comes the boil. Boil for 1 minute then remove the pan from the heat and leave to cool completely.

Strain the oil through a fine mesh sieve/strainer, pour into a sterilized glass bottle and seal. Keep in the fridge for up to 1 month and use as required.

Garlic oil Asia

This oil (opposite, right) is particularly good drizzled over noodles but as it doesn't keep as well as chilli/chile oil, I make less and use it up within two weeks. Store in the fridge.

1 whole head garlic
125 ml/½ cup peanut oil
sterilized glass bottle with
  an airtight cap

Makes 125 ml/½ cup

Peel each garlic clove and cut into 3-mm/⅛-in. slices.

Put the peanut oil in a small saucepan and set over a low heat until shimmering. Add the garlic slices and cook for about 20 minutes until they are crisp and golden but not burnt.

Remove the garlic with a slotted spoon and drain on paper towels. Reserve the oil, straining several times through a fine mesh sieve/strainer to discard any small bits of garlic and set aside to cool completely. Pour into a sterilized glass bottle and seal. Keep in the fridge for up to 2 weeks and use as required.

TIP: The garlic slices can be used in salads or as a soup topping, but will only keep for a few days in the fridge.

Chicken stock Asia

Chicken stock (opposite, left) is used extensively throughout Asia with the exception of Japan and Korea where dashi is more commonly used, although you will find it in some dishes. Unlike Western stocks, the flavour tends to be more intense with a pleasing hint of garlic and ginger.

2 kg/4 lbs. chicken pieces,
  preferably free range
a bunch of spring onions/
  scallions, trimmed and
  chopped
1 whole head garlic, cloves
  roughly chopped
5 cm/2 in. fresh ginger, peeled,
  sliced and pounded
1 red onion, roughly chopped
salt, to taste

Makes 2 litres/3½ pints

Put the chicken pieces in a large saucepan with the spring onions/scallions, garlic, ginger and red onion and pour over 3 litres/5¼ pints cold water. Set the pan over a medium heat and bring the mixture slowly to the boil, skimming the surface to remove any scum. Reduce the heat and simmer gently for 1½ hours until the stock is full of flavour.

Strain and discard the chicken pieces (I like to taste the chicken to see how much flavour is retained and use it in sandwiches if still tasty) and vegetables. Return the stock to the pan and simmer until reduced to 2 litres/3½ pints. Add a little salt to taste.

Use immediately or cool and chill overnight. The stock will keep, stored in an airtight container, for 3 days in the fridge or can be frozen for up to 1 month. Skim off any residual fat from the top before using each time.

Dashi broth Japan

Dashi (opposite, right) is a Japanese stock and forms the underbelly of many Japanese dishes. Dried kombu or 'kelp' is simmered in water and then dried bonito flakes are added to give the stock a very distinctive smokey flavour and sea-water aroma.

15 g/1 tablespoon chopped
  dried kombu (see page 20)
15 g/1 tablespoon dried bonito
  flakes (see page 21)

Makes 1 litre/1¾ pints

Pour 1.25 litres/2 pints cold water into a saucepan, add the kombu and set aside for 30 minutes to soften. Bring the mixture to the boil over a medium heat, removing any scum that appears on the surface, then reduce the heat and simmer gently for 10 minutes.

Remove the pan from the heat, stir in the bonito flakes and allow the broth to cool. Strain with a fine mesh sieve/strainer and use immediately or chill until required. The broth will keep stored in an airtight container for 3 days in the fridge or can be frozen for up to 1 month.

TIP: For a vegetarian option, omit the bonito flakes and increase the kombu to a total of 20 g/1 tablespoon.

CHINESE

50 ml/¼ cup light soy sauce

2 teaspoons Chinese black vinegar

1 teaspoon caster/granulated sugar

1 teaspoon freshly grated root ginger

1 teaspoon sesame oil

¼ teaspoon chilli/chile oil (see page 22)

Makes 75 ml/scant ⅓ cup

JAPANESE

200 ml/¾ cup dashi broth (see page 25)

3 tablespoons Japanese soy sauce

3 tablespoons mirin

½ teaspoon caster/granulated sugar

Makes 300 ml/1¼ cups

sterilized glass jars with airtight lids

1 teaspoon sea salt

1 teaspoon freshly ground black pepper

1 lime, cut into wedges

Makes 75 ml/scant ⅓ cup

Dipping sauces China and Japan

These two dipping sauces (opposite, top and bottom-right) are perfect for serving with all manner of noodle dishes. The Chinese chilli/chile soy and vinegar version is a perfect sauce for wontons, steamed or fried, as well as other noodle dishes, while the Japanese version is traditionally served in hot summer months with chilled noodles.

For each sauce, whisk all the ingredients together in a bowl, or, if you have a clean glass jar with a lid, put all the ingredients into the jar, screw on the lid and shake well.

Serve immediately or store in a glass jar with an airtight lid in the fridge. The Chinese sauce will keep for up to 5 days but you can store the Japanese sauce in the fridge until it is all used up.

Yin yang lime juice Vietnam

Vietnamese cuisine is based on the yin and yang philosophy, where balance is integral to the flavour of a dish, as well as life. This (opposite, bottom-left) is a great example of the principle.

Make separate piles of salt and pepper on opposite sides of the same dish. Squeeze the juice from the lime over each pile. Using a chopstick or small spoon, mix the salt with a little of the juice and then mix the pepper in the same way to make a black paste and a white paste.

Shape into a yin yang symbol and serve.

Balachung Myanmar

A must-have condiment in Burmese cooking, this salty, spicy, crispy dish (opposite, front) is served with almost every meal. It is delicious strewn over any noodle dish.

50 g/¼ cup dried shrimp (see
    page 21)
6 tablespoons peanut (or
    vegetable) oil
2 Asian shallots (see page 16),
    thinly sliced
2 garlic cloves, sliced
5 cm/2 in. fresh ginger, peeled
    and thinly sliced
2–3 teaspoons dried red
    chilli/hot red pepper flakes
1 tablespoon shrimp paste (see
    page 21)

Makes about 55 g/¼ cup

Grind the dried shrimp to a paste using a spice grinder or pestle and mortar and set aside.

Heat the oil in a wok set over a medium–high heat and fry the shallots for 4–5 minutes, until crisp and golden. Remove the shallots from the oil using a slotted spoon and drain on paper towels, leaving the pan over the heat.

Add the garlic, ginger and chilli/hot red pepper flakes to the hot oil and cook for 2–3 minutes, until crisp and golden. Remove with a slotted spoon and drain on paper towels, again leaving the pan over the heat.

Stir in the ground dried shrimp and the shrimp paste and stir-fry for 2–3 minutes, until fragrant. Return the shallots and garlic mixture to the pan and stir gently until you a have a slightly sticky mixture. Cool completely before scattering over your favourite noodle dish.

The balachung can be stored in an airtight container for up to 2 weeks.

Deep-fried shallots Thailand

Like balachung, deep-fried shallots (opposite, back) are an integral part of Thai, as well as Vietnamese, Cambodian and Laotian cuisine, where they are sprinkled over numerous salads, soups, rice and noodle dishes. You can buy these from Asian stores but I like to make my own.

12 Asian shallots (see page
    16), thinly sliced
vegetable oil, for deep frying

Makes about 50 g/⅓ cup

Pour the oil into a wok or (old) saucepan about 5 cm/2 in. up the side of the pan and set over a medium heat. Test the temperature of the pan by dropping a cube of bread into the hot oil – it should crisp within 30 seconds.

Deep-fry the shallots, in batches, for 2–3 minutes, until crisp and golden, but do not allow the shallots to burn or they will become bitter. Remove with a slotted spoon and drain on paper towels.

Serve immediately or store in an airtight container for up to 2 weeks. If they become a little soggy, crisp them up in a dry frying pan/skillet as necessary.

TIP: Strain the leftover shallot oil through a fine mesh sieve/strainer and use in salads and stir-fries.

Asian pickles Japan, Korea and China

A mainstay of Asian cooking, in Japan, pickles are eaten as a snack, while in China they are commonly served with noodle soups and salads. Kimchi, a spiced pickled cabbage, is the national dish of Korea and is served with every meal.

Pickled cucumber Japan

2 teaspoons salt
3 tablespoons caster/ granulated
  sugar
3 small cucumbers
2 x 500 ml/1 pint sterilized glass
  jars with airtight lids

Makes 2 jars

Combine the salt and sugar
in a plastic container. Cut the
cucumbers into 3-mm/⅛-in. thick
slices on the diagonal and add to
the salt mixture, stirring well to coat
evenly. Seal the container and store
in the fridge for 3 days.

Remove from the fridge and taste a
piece of cucumber to see if you like
the pickle flavour. You can use
immediately or continue to pickle
them for a further day or two.

Pickled vegetables China

300 ml/1¼ cups white vinegar
200 g/1 cup caster/granulated
  sugar
1½ teaspoons salt
1 large carrot, cut into batons
1 celery stick, trimmed and cut
  into batons
½ cucumber, deseeded and cut
  into batons
a 500 ml/1 pint sterilized glass
  jar with an airtight lid

Makes 1 jar

Put the vinegar, sugar and salt
in a saucepan set over a low heat
and warm through until the sugar
is dissolved. Increase the heat,
bring the mixture to the boil,
simmer for 1 minute then remove
from the heat.

Put the prepared vegetables in
a large mixing bowl and pour over
the syrup. Set aside until
completely cool. Store in the fridge
until ready to serve. These pickles
can be made up to 3 days ahead.

Quick kimchi Korea

350 g/6 cups Chinese cabbage,
  thinly sliced
4 teaspoons sea salt
2 tablespoons caster/ granulated
  sugar
1 tablespoon dried Korean chilli
  flakes (see page 156)
2 teaspoons freshly grated ginger
2 garlic cloves, crushed
2 tablespoons fish sauce
2 teaspoons sesame seeds, toasted
2 spring onions/scallions, trimmed
  and thinly sliced
a 500 ml/1 pint sterilized glass
  jar with an airtight lid

Makes 1 jar

Put the cabbage in a bowl and
stir in the salt. Add enough water
to cover and leave to soak for
30 minutes. Drain well and squeeze
out excess water using a clean
kitchen cloth.

Mix together the sugar, chilli/hot
red pepper flakes, ginger, garlic,
fish sauce and sesame seeds in
a small bowl to make a thin paste.
Stir the paste into the cabbage with
the spring onions/scallions, cover
and leave to marinate for 1 hour.
Serve, or store for up to 2 days
in the fridge.

Wafu dressing Japan

1 small shallot, very finely
   chopped
2 tablespoons Japanese soy
   sauce
2 tablespoons rice wine
   vinegar
2 tablespoons Dashi broth (see
   page 25)
2 teaspoons sesame oil
2 teaspoons caster/granulated
   sugar
1 teaspoon freshly grated
   ginger
½ teaspoon crushed garlic

Makes 150 ml/²/₃ cup

Literally translated as 'Japanese-style', wafu is a soy,
vinegar and sesame dressing (opposite, top) to which other
flavourings can be added. It is delicious drizzled over simple
leaf salads or more complex noodle salads and is a great recipe
to have in your culinary arsenal.

Put all the ingredients in a sterilized glass jar, screw the lid on tightly and
shake well until amalgamated.

Use as required. The dressing will keep in the fridge for up to 5 days.

Szechuan chilli dressing China

100 ml/⅓ cup sunflower oil
1–2 teaspoons dried red
   chilli/hot red pepper flakes
2 tablespoons light soy sauce
1 tablespoon black vinegar
2 teaspoons caster/granulated
   sugar
¼ teaspoon Szechuan
   peppercorns (see page 19)

Makes 200 ml/¾ cup

The perfect sauce (opposite, bottom) for dipping hot steamed
and fried wontons into.

Heat the oil in a small saucepan set over a medium heat until it just starts to
shimmer. Remove from the heat and stir in the chilli/hot red pepper flakes. Set
aside for 30 minutes, then strain through a fine mesh sieve/strainer into a clean
bowl. Stir in the remaining ingredients and serve as required.

TIP: If you are making this dressing ahead of time omit the peppercorns and
add just before serving.

Korean dipping sauces Korea

Korea is famed for its love of the condiment or side dish. Choganjang is the simplest of dipping sauces (opposite, top-left), perfect with all noodle dishes. If you prefer your sauces spicy, try Cho-gochujang (opposite top-right) – you can increase the amount of chilli/chile paste you use, but I find the heat in this sweet and spicy chilli dipping sauce works for me. Ssamjang is a spicy fermented chilli bean paste (opposite, bottom), often served with Korean BBQ, but also delicious stirred into Korean soups.

Choganjang Korea

2 tablespoons dark soy sauce
1 tablespoon brown rice vinegar
a pinch of sesame seeds, toasted

Makes 45 ml/3 tablespoons

Pour the soy sauce and vinegar into a small bowl and sprinkle with a few sesame seeds.

Use as required or store the soy and vinegar mixture without the sesame seeds in a sterilized glass bottle until ready to serve.

Cho-gochujang Korea

1 tablespoon sesame seeds
1–2 teaspoons gochujang (see page 156)
2 tablespoons rice wine vinegar
2 tablespoons dark soy sauce
1 tablespoon clear honey
2 teaspoons sesame oil
1 spring onion/scallion, trimmed and finely chopped
1 garlic clove, crushed

Makes 150 ml/²⁄₃ cup

Dry-fry the sesame seeds in a small frying pan/skillet set over a medium heat until evenly toasted. Transfer to a spice grinder or pestle and mortar and grind to a rough paste.

Put the ground sesame seeds in a small bowl and stir in the gochujang, vinegar, soy sauce, honey and sesame oil until smooth, then add the spring onion/scallion and garlic and stir well. Serve immediately.

Ssamjang Korea

60 ml/4 tablespoons doenjang (see page 156)
2 teaspoons gochujang (see page 156)
1 spring onion/scallion, trimmed and finely chopped
1 small garlic clove, crushed
1 Asian shallot, finely chopped
2 teaspoons rice wine
2 teaspoons sesame oil
1 teaspoon clear honey
1 teaspoon sesame seeds, toasted

Makes 150 ml/²⁄₃ cup

Put all the ingredients in a small bowl and use as required.

Alternatively, transfer to a plastic container, seal and store in the fridge for up to 3 days.

Nuoc cham Vietnam

2 large red chillies/chiles,
  chopped
2 red bird's eye chillies/chiles,
  deseeded and chopped
2 garlic cloves, crushed
4 tablespoons grated palm
  sugar (see page 21)
4 tablespoons Thai fish sauce
grated zest and freshly
  squeezed juice of 4 limes
salt and pepper

**Makes about 100 ml/scant
  ½ cup**

A classic Vietnamese sauce (opposite, right) served with everything from salads and soups to stir-fries. There are countless variations of this sauce but all are hot, salty, sweet and sour – flavours so beloved in South-east Asia. This version is tempered to my taste, but feel free to add more chilli/chile if you enjoy a hotter flavour.

Put the chillies/chiles, garlic and palm sugar in a pestle and mortar or food processor and pound or blend to form a paste. Transfer to a mixing bowl and whisk in the remaining ingredients.

Store in an airtight container in the fridge and use as required.

Green nam jim Thailand

2 green bird's eye chillies/
  chiles, deseeded and
  roughly chopped
4 garlic cloves, chopped
a large pinch of salt
2 tablespoons chopped fresh
  coriander/cilantro
4 tablespoons grated palm
  sugar (see page 21)
4 tablespoons fish sauce
4 tablespoons freshly
  squeezed lime juice

**Makes about 100 ml/scant
  ½ cup**

The Thai equivalent to nuoc cham, I like to make nam jim (opposite, left) with green chillies/chiles for a striking contrast to the Vietnamese alternative, but red or green can be used, as desired.

Put the chilli/chile, garlic and salt in a pestle and mortar or food processor and pound or blend to form a paste. Transfer to a mixing bowl and stir in the coriander/cilantro, palm sugar, fish sauce and lime juice, and stir until the sugar is dissolved.

Store in an airtight container in the fridge and use as required.

Sambal olek Malaysia

This chilli/chile sauce (opposite, left) has a lovely depth of flavour to it with a hint of tamarind, which is very fragrant – perfect with salads and soups.

5 Asian shallots (see page 16), chopped
25 g/scant ¼ cup chopped large red chillies/chiles (deseeded, if desired)
2 large garlic cloves, sliced
1 lemon grass stalk, trimmed and chopped
1 teaspoon ground turmeric
2 tablespoons peanut oil
1 tablespoon tamarind paste (see page 21)
1 tablespoon light soy sauce
1 tablespoon caster/ granulated sugar
salt, to taste (optional)

Makes 125 ml/½ cup

Put the shallots, chillies/chiles, garlic, lemon grass and turmeric in a food processor and blend until smooth, adding 2 teaspoons of the oil if necessary.

Heat the remaining oil in a wok or large frying pan/skillet set over a very low heat and gently fry the paste for about 10 minutes, until really fragrant. Stir in the tamarind paste, soy sauce and sugar and cook, stirring continuously, for 5 minutes until the oil comes to the top.

Remove the pan from the heat and leave to cool completely. Use as required or store in a sterilized glass bottle or jar in the fridge for up to 1 month.

Sweet and sour chilli sauce Myanmar

This Burmese chilli/chile dressing (opposite, right) is a simpler affair, but delicious nonetheless. I love it drizzled into soups but be sure to make plenty if you have a taste for it – you'll soon be adding a dash to every meal.

15 g/3 tablespoons chopped dried red chillies/chiles
4 garlic cloves, roughly chopped
2 tablespoons fish sauce
2 tablespoons soft brown sugar
50 ml/scant ¼ cup rice vinegar

Makes 250 ml/1 cup

Roughly crush the chillies/chiles in a pestle and mortar and transfer to a small saucepan with 75 ml/scant ⅓ cup cold water. Bring the mixture to the boil and simmer very gently over a low heat for 2 minutes, add the garlic and cook for a further 3 minutes.

Transfer the mixture to a food processor with the fish sauce and sugar, and blend until smooth. Add the vinegar and blend again.

Pour the sauce into a sterilized glass bottle and seal. Store in the fridge for 2–3 days before using and then up to 1 month.

Tirk salouk swai Cambodia

1 large mango, peeled and
chopped
freshly squeezed juice of
½ lime
1 spring onion/scallion,
trimmed and finely chopped
2 tablespoons chopped fresh
coriander/cilantro
1–2 large green chillies/chiles,
deseeded and finely
chopped
1–2 teaspoons fish sauce,
to taste

Serves 4

Much like the salsas of Mexico, the Caribbean and South America, this mango salsa (opposite, front) makes use of the seasonal glut of fresh mangoes. It is at once sweet, salty and sour – quite delicious and lovely served alongside a seafood or chicken noodle salad.

Put the mango flesh, lime juice, spring onion/scallion, coriander/cilantro and chillies/chiles into a small mixing bowl, stir well and season with fish sauce to taste.

Serve at once.

Jeow marg leng Laos

A cooked tomato salsa (opposite, back) that is wonderfully spicy and smokey. It works well stirred into soups or alongside noodle salads.

6 large cherry tomatoes
6 garlic cloves, unpeeled
1 large shallot, unpeeled
1–2 small red bird's eye
chillies/chiles
½ teaspoon caster/granulated
sugar
1 spring onion/scallion,
trimmed and finely chopped
1 tablespoon chopped fresh
coriander/cilantro
2 teaspoons freshly squeezed
lime juice
1 teaspoon fish sauce

Serves 4

Heat a stovetop ridged grill pan over a medium heat until smoking and then grill the tomatoes for 15–20 minutes until completely charred and softened. Set aside to cool, then peel and discard the blackened skin.

Repeat with the garlic cloves, whole shallot and chillies/chiles, cooking them until the skins are charred and the flesh softened. Allow them to cool, then peel and discard the skin. Chop the vegetables and put in a pestle and mortar. Pound to a rough paste.

Transfer the paste to a mixing bowl and stir in the sugar, spring onion/scallion, coriander/cilantro, lime juice and fish sauce. Store in a sterilized glass jar in the fridge for up to 3 weeks and use as required.

small dishes and bites

Small dishes and bites

The structure of meals in Asia and South-east Asia differs to those in the West and meals tend to be larger family affairs with lots of small dishes making up one course or people will 'graze' on smaller bites throughout the day. What we in Europe and America think of as starters or appetizers, don't really exist, however there are simply hundreds of little dishes often made and sold as snacks by street hawkers that lend themselves perfectly to be served and as an appetizer before a main course.

I love starters/appetizers, and when I eat out at Asian restaurants it is these smaller dishes that are the most exciting part of the menu for me. I often find it almost impossible to choose just one dish, so much so that I frequently order half a dozen little dishes rather than one main meal. Crispy fried spring rolls, glutinous mouth-watering dumplings in a spicy chilli/chile sauce or perhaps a burst of fragrant herbs in a summer roll all sound so tempting.

I wanted to include the following recipes as starters/appetizers so they fit in with the way I like to eat when I have friends over. Start with something small but perfectly formed with a glass of deliciously chilled white wine, perhaps Steamed rice noodle dumplings with scallops (see page 46), before moving on to the main event, which could be one main/entrée dish or a combination of two or three smaller dishes, depending on how many people you are cooking for or just what you fancy.

You could of course make half a dozen or so of these starters/appetizers to serve together as a more typical Asian-style meal. If you do, think about different textures with a selection of meat, fish and vegetable dishes with perhaps a Thai Mee grob (see page 65), Noodle-wrapped prawns/shrimp with chilli and garlic sauce (see page 62) then Salmon gyozas (see page 57), finishing up with the BBQ pork noodle bowls with dipping sauce (see page 58) or Beef bulgogi and rice noodle wraps (see page 53).

Although not strictly noodles, dumplings fit very comfortably into this book. The dough used to make them is the same as the dough used in noodle making. Wonton dough is made with eggs and flour and gyoza dough is just flour and water. You can make them at home, but I find the bought wrappers so convenient (and they freeze very well) so I prefer to use these and recommend you do so too.

We can follow the fascinating migration of culinary dishes by looking at the different dumpling and wrapper recipes from China through Japan and down into South-east Asia. The Chinese serve lots of different types of dumplings usually at yum cha (tea time) or dim sum, depending on where you live. Wonton wrappers are generally used to make steamed or boiled dumplings whereas gyoza wrappers – or 'jiaozi' – the Chinese name for this popular dumpling – are more commonly braised in a little water and then fried until the bases are crispy. These have morphed into what are called 'pot stickers' in the US. Fillings vary but are frequently meat or seafood or a combination of the two. So although strictly speaking the two types of wrappers are used to make different dumplings they are actually interchangeable and you could use either type if pressed and availability is limited.

In Vietnam, rice paper wrappers are far more common and are always made with dried wrappers rehydrated in warm water to soften them enough to roll. They come in small or large sheets and can be filled with a whole host of ingredients but usually contain cooked vermicelli noodles, shredded or pickled vegetables, pork or prawn/shrimp and beansprouts. They can be served with different sauces depending on the region and I have added my own version of this delicious dish with smoked duck, fresh herbs and vegetables, served with a Hoisin and peanut dipping sauce (see page 58). Deep-fried spring rolls, often vegetarian (see page 66) can be found in different guises the length and breadth of Asia, some better than others. Mine, of course, are yummy!

To add an extra dimension, noodles are great deep-fried until crispy. Firstly they are rehydrated and left to dry thoroughly before being deep-fried until crisp. This adds a fantastic crunch to dishes especially when sprinkled on top of a soup or salad. Try the classic Thai dish of deep-fried crispy rice noodles with a hot, sweet and salty sauce called Mee grob (see page 65).

Of course you need to be careful when deep-frying any foods, so I recommend a large deep wok filled to about 5 cm/2 in. with vegetable or sunflower oil. Preferably use a sugar thermometer to test the heat is 160–200°C (325–400°F), but generally the oil is at the optimum temperature when a small cube of bread dropped into the oil crisps and turns brown in 20–30 seconds. Always deep-fry ingredients in batches so things cook evenly and do not lower the heat of the oil too much.

When I return to Asia after a long gap between visits, it is the hustle and bustle of walking down streets heaving with local people simply going about their daily lives that I find myself drawn to. This is the place where I believe you get to the soul of this vibrant region with its fascinating history and often closely linked cultural heritage.

Here you are bombarded with the sights and sounds, smells and textures of everyday life and right at the heart of this is the food. Everywhere you look people are cooking, buying, eating and arguing over food at street stalls, market stalls and makeshift restaurants. It might not appear organized to the traveller simply passing through, but it is and it is here that I return to time and time again to remind myself of what I have been missing since my last visit. I'm there to observe, to enjoy, to learn, to smile and most of all to eat.

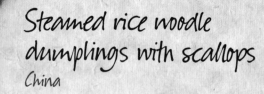

Steamed rice noodle dumplings with scallops
China

I love steamed dumplings and these are just about my favourite type. Dim sum or 'yum cha', as it's known in Australia, was always a favourite lunch out for us – officious waiters pushing trolleys with towering bamboo steamers full of different dumplings and other delights.

250 g/½ lb. scallops (without corals)
50 g/1½ oz. (about 6) water
    chestnuts, drained and chopped
2 garlic cloves, crushed
1 tablespoon freshly chopped garlic
    chives (see page 18)
1 tablespoon light soy sauce
2 teaspoons oyster sauce
1 teaspoon sesame oil
24 wonton wrappers

3–4 tablespoons sunflower oil
Szechuan chilli dressing (see page 33)
spring onions/scallions, thinly sliced
    to garnish

*a baking sheet lined with baking
    parchment*
a medium bamboo steamer

Serves 4

Begin by preparing the scallops, cutting away the grey muscle attached at one side and chop into small cubes. Put the scallop meat into a bowl with the chestnuts, garlic, garlic chives, soy sauce, oyster sauce and sesame oil, and stir.

Lay the wonton wrappers flat on a board and place a teaspoon of the scallop mixture in the centre. Brush around the edges with a little water and draw the sides up and around the filling, pressing the edges together to seal. Transfer each one to the prepared baking sheet.

Dip the base of each dumpling in sunflower oil and transfer to the bamboo steamer. Cover and steam over a pan of simmering water for 10–12 minutes until firm and cooked through.

Serve with the dressing, garnished with shredded spring onions/scallions.

Chinese pot stickers China

Not to be confused with wontons, pot stickers, as they are called in North America, are a form of Chinese dumpling that is fried, steamed and then fried again so they are at once both soft and crispy. I find it best to use a non-stick frying pan/skillet to make these rather than a wok as you need an even base for the oil to settle.

125 g/2 cups finely chopped Chinese cabbage

1 teaspoon salt

1 leek, trimmed and finely chopped

2 garlic cloves, crushed

2 tablespoons freshly chopped coriander/cilantro

250 g/1 cup minced pork

24 gyoza wrappers (see page 13)

2 tablespoons vegetable oil

1 quantity Chilli, soy and vinegar dipping sauce (see page 26)

garlic chive flowers (see page 19), to garnish (optional)

a baking sheet lined with baking parchment

Serves 4

Put the cabbage in a large mixing bowl with the salt and toss well to coat. Transfer to a colander and leave to drain for 1 hour to remove as much water as possible from the cabbage. Squeeze out any remaining water and put the cabbage in a clean large mixing bowl with the leek, garlic and coriander/cilantro. Gradually work in the minced pork until combined.

Working one at a time, lay the gyoza wrappers out flat and place a teaspoon of the mixture on one half of each wrapper. Dampen the edges with a little cold water, fold the wrapper over the filling and carefully press the edges together to seal.

Preheat the oven to 110°C (225°F) Gas ¼ (or the lowest heat setting).

Heat 1 tablespoon of the oil in a wok or large non-stick frying pan/skillet set over a high heat. Add half the dumplings and fry for about 1 minute until the bottoms are golden. Add 100 ml/⅓ cup water and simmer, partially covered, for 5 minutes, until the water has evaporated. Cook for a further 2–3 minutes until the bottoms are crispy. Transfer the dumplings to the prepared baking sheet, turn off the oven and set in the still-warm oven while you cook the remaining dumplings in the same way.

Arrange the dumplings on plates and serve drizzled with the dipping sauce. Garnish with garlic chive flowers, if wished, and serve.

Kimchi noodle dumplings with dipping sauce Korea

Before I'd eaten Kimchi, I always imagined fermented cabbage to be rather scary and even a little unpalatable, but in fact it is delicious, as are these crispy-bottomed dumplings. Traditionally Kimchi is quite fiery so I have used just one tablespoon of chilli/hot red pepper flakes, which is far less than you will find in most Korean recipes. Add more if you dare!

150 g/⅔ cup minced pork
150 g/scant 1 cup cooked prawns/shrimp, peeled and very finely chopped
100 g/4 oz. Quick kimchi (see page 30)
2 teaspoons dark soy sauce
½ beaten egg
20 gyoza wrappers (see page 13)
4 tablespoons vegetable oil

TO SERVE
1 quantity Choganjang (see page 34)
spring onions/scallions, thinly sliced
a baking sheet lined with baking parchment

Serves 4

Put the pork, prawns/shrimp, kimchi, soy sauce and beaten egg in a large mixing bowl and mix together until evenly combined.

Working one at a time, lay the gyoza wrappers out flat and place a teaspoon of the mixture on one half of each wrapper. Dampen the edges with a little cold water, fold the wrapper over the filling and carefully press the edges together to seal.

Preheat the oven to 110°C (225°F) Gas ¼ (or the lowest heat setting).

Heat the oil in a wok or large non-stick frying pan/skillet set over a high heat. Add half the dumplings and fry for about 1 minute until the bottoms are golden. Add 125 ml/½ cup water to the pan, cover and simmer for 5 minutes until the filling is heated through. Remove the lid and cook for a further 1–2 minutes until the bottoms are crispy. Transfer the dumplings to the prepared baking sheet, turn off the oven and set in the still-warm oven while you cook the remaining dumplings in the same way.

Arrange the dumplings on warmed plates and serve with the choganjang, scattered with spring onions/scallions.

Beef bulgogi and rice noodle wraps Korea

The word bulgogi means 'fire meat' and refers to marinated and grilled meats, usually beef. Here it is stir-fried and combined with shiitake mushrooms and Korean sweet potato noodles, wrapped in lettuce leaves and topped with kimchi and ssamjang.

500 g/1 lb. beef rib-eye steak

2 tablespoons light or dark soy sauce

2 tablespoons soft brown sugar

1 Asian shallot (see page 16), finely chopped

1 garlic clove, crushed

2 teaspoons sesame oil, plus extra for dressing

½ teaspoon Chinese five-spice powder

125 g/4 oz. sweet potato noodles (see page 15)

2 tablespoons peanut oil

125 g/4 oz. shiitake mushrooms, trimmed and cut into quarters

4 tablespoons Quick kimchi (optional, page 30)

Ssamjang sauce (see page 34)

Serves 4

Begin by preparing the beef. Thinly slice the steak and arrange in a single layer in a wide, shallow dish. Combine the soy sauce, sugar, shallot, garlic, sesame oil and Chinese five-spice powder, and pour over the beef. Set aside to marinate for at least 1 hour.

Plunge the sweet potato noodles into a pan of boiling water and cook for 4–5 minutes until al dente. Drain, refresh under cold water and drain again. Shake the noodles dry and dress with a little sesame oil to prevent them from sticking together. Set aside.

Heat the oil in a wok or large frying pan/skillet set over a medium heat until it starts to shimmer. Add the beef in batches and stir-fry for 2–3 minutes until golden. Remove with a slotted spoon. Add the mushrooms and any remaining marinade and stir-fry for 1 minute. Return the beef to the pan along with the noodles and stir-fry for 1 minute, until everything is heated through.

Divide the beef noodles between bowls and serve with lettuce leaves, kimchi and the ssamjang sauce. Wrap, roll and eat.

Salmon and scallion gyoza Japan

Japanese food is hugely popular in Sydney and many neighbourhoods have at least one, if not more than one, Japanese restaurant. This recipe is from one such restaurant called Moshi Moshi close to the Northern beaches.

250 g/9 oz. skinless salmon fillet, boned
2 spring onions/scallions, trimmed and
   thinly sliced
1 tablespoon mirin
1 tablespoon light soy sauce
20 gyoza wrappers (see page 13)
1 tablespoon grapeseed oil

½ quantity Japanese dipping sauce
   (see page 26)
black sesame seeds and micro herbs,
   to serve

a baking sheet lined with baking parchment

Serves 4

Begin by preparing the salmon. Cut the fillet into small cubes and put in a large mixing bowl. Add the spring onions/scallions, mirin and soy sauce, and stir well to combine.

Working one at a time, lay the gyoza wrappers out flat and place a teaspoon of the mixture on one half of each wrapper. Dampen the edges with a little cold water, fold the wrapper over the filling and carefully press the edges together to seal.

Preheat the oven to 110°C (225°F) Gas ¼ (or the lowest heat setting).

Heat the oil in a wok or large non-stick frying pan/skillet over a medium heat and fry half the gyoza on one side until really browned. Add 100 ml/⅓ cup water and simmer, partially covered, for 3 minutes until the water is evaporated. Fry for a further minute until crisp. Transfer the gyoza to the prepared baking sheet, turn off the oven and set in the still-warm oven while you cook the remaining gyoza in the same way.

Arrange the cooked gyoza on serving dishes and drizzle over the dipping sauce. Sprinkle with sesame seeds and micro herbs, and serve immediately.

Chilled soba noodles with dipping sauce *Japan*

In marked contrast to other Asian cuisines, Japanese dishes are far simpler in their design and composition, with delicate flavours balanced perfectly. This dish of chilled noodles is traditionally served with three small cubes of ice in the middle to accentuate the cold. It would be eaten in the summer months only.

250 g/9 oz. dried soba noodles (see page 12)
2 spring onions/scallions, thinly sliced
2 teaspoons freshly grated ginger
2 teaspoons wasabi paste (see page 157)
a 5-cm/2-in. square of dried nori (see page 157)

1 quantity Japanese dipping sauce (see page 26)
12 ice cubes, to serve

Serves 4

Plunge the noodles into a large saucepan of boiling water and return to the boil. Cook for 4–5 minutes until the noodles are tender. Drain well and refresh under cold water stirring until the noodles separate and the starch is removed. Drain again and leave to dry on a clean kitchen cloth until required.

For each serving, arrange a pile of spring onions/scallions, a little of the grated ginger, a little wasabi, a pinch of the nori strips and a bowl of the dipping sauce. Divide the noodles between small bowls and place 3 ice cubes in the middle of each one.

Serve with the plated garnishes and enjoy.

BBQ pork noodle bowls with dipping sauce Vietnam

In all Asian dishes you will find a lovely balance of strong and delicate flavours. Here we have the richness of pork belly, the mellow flavour of noodles, the zing of pickled vegetables and finally a sweet, sour dressing.

500 g/1 lb. pork belly strips, each cut into 3 pieces
3 tablespoons fish sauce
2 tablespoons ketjap manis (see page 156)
1 teaspoon Chinese five-spice powder
½ teaspoon freshly ground black pepper
4 garlic cloves, crushed
250 g/9 oz. dried rice stick noodles (see page 14)
125 g/2⅓ cups beansprouts, trimmed

8–12 cup-shaped leaves from an iceberg/butter lettuce
a selection of fresh herbs, such as mint, coriander/cilantro and Thai basil
1 quantity Pickled vegetables (see page 30)
1 quantity Nuoc cham (see page 37)

a roasting pan lined with baking parchment

Serves 4

Place the pork belly in a shallow dish. Whisk the fish sauce, ketjap manis, spice, pepper and garlic cloves together, and pour over the pork. Cover and set in the fridge to marinate overnight.

Preheat the oven to 180°C (350°F) Gas 4.

Transfer the pork belly to the prepared roasting pan and roast in the preheated oven for 1 hour, turning halfway through, until the pork is golden, sticky and tender. Leave to cool for 30 minutes until just warm and cut into pieces.

Meanwhile, put the noodles in a bowl, cover with boiling water and soak for 30 minutes until softened. Drain the noodles, pat dry and divide between serving bowls. Arrange the pork, beansprouts, lettuce leaves, herbs and pickled vegetables on plates around the table for people to help themselves.

Serve with a bowl of nuoc cham.

Smoked duck rice paper rolls Vietnam

Fresh spring rolls, often called 'summer rolls' due to their refreshing nature, are typically served in summer months and can have many different fillings. I have adapted this recipe to use smoked duck breast (available from specialist food stores), which adds a further intriguing flavour to these delicious rolls.

100 g/3½ oz. rice vermicelli
    noodles (see page 14)
2 teaspoons fish sauce
2 teaspoons freshly squeezed
    lime juice
2 teaspoons caster/granulated
    sugar
8 x 20-cm/8-in. dried rice
    paper wrappers (see pages
    14–15)
100 g/3½ oz. smoked duck
    breast (see Tip)
100 g/3 cups thinly sliced
    lettuce
1 carrot, peeled and cut into
    thin batons
½ cucumber, deseeded and cut
    into batons
20 fresh Thai basil leaves

**HOISIN AND PEANUT DIPPING
    SAUCE**
2 tablespoons hoisin sauce
1 tablespoon smooth peanut
    butter
1 tablespoon warm water
2 teaspoons freshly squeezed
    lime juice
1 teaspoon dark soy sauce
¼ teaspoon caster/granulated
    sugar

Serves 4

Put the noodles in a bowl, cover with boiling water and soak for 30 minutes until softened. Drain the noodles, pat dry and transfer to a large mixing bowl. Whisk the fish sauce, lime juice and sugar together until the sugar is dissolved and pour over the noodles. Toss well and set aside.

Next make the dipping sauce. Put all the ingredients in a small saucepan set over a low heat. Heat gently, stirring until the peanut butter is softened and the sauce smooth. Remove from the heat and set aside to cool.

Working one at a time, dip the rice paper wrappers into a bowl of warm water for about a minute until softened and then pat dry on paper towels. Lay each wrapper out flat and top with a few noodles, the smoked duck slices, shredded lettuce, carrot, cucumber and basil leaves. Fold the ends of the rice paper over the filling and then roll up tightly to form parcels.

Serve with the dipping sauce.

TIP: If you can't find smoked duck you could use smoked salmon or smoked trout intead.

Noodle-wrapped prawns with chilli and garlic sauce Thailand

A great use of both noodles and prawns/shrimp these make a lovely canapé or finger food. I first ate noodle-wrapped prawns/shrimp in Phuket town, away from the busy touristy beach area, where there are some lovely authentic Thai restaurants.

100 g/3½ oz. dried thin egg noodles (see page 13)
24 large prawns/shrimp, peeled and de-veined
vegetable oil, for deep frying

SWEET CHILLI SAUCE
2 heads of garlic, cloves peeled
¼ teaspoon salt
6 long red chillies/chiles, deseeded
4 tablespoons caster/ granulated sugar
2 tablespoons rice wine vinegar
1 teaspoon light soy sauce

a baking sheet lined with baking parchment

Serves 4

Start by making the sauce. Put all the ingredients in a saucepan set over a medium heat and bring to the boil, stirring to dissolve the sugar. Reduce the heat, cover and simmer gently for 15 minutes until the garlic is tender. Cool slightly, then transfer the mixture to a food processor. Blend until smooth and return the mixture to the pan. Simmer uncovered for a further 10–15 minutes until the sauce is thick and glossy. Remove from the heat and set aside to cool.

Put the noodles in a bowl, cover with boiling water and soak for 20 minutes until softened. Drain the noodles and pat dry with paper towels. Wrap 8–10 noodles around each prawn/shrimp and set aside.

Preheat the oven to 110°C (225°F) Gas ¼ (or the lowest heat setting).

Pour vegetable oil into a wok or large saucepan to reach about 5 cm/2 in. up the side and set over a medium–high heat. Heat until a cube of bread dropped into the oil crisps in 30 seconds. Deep-fry the wrapped prawns/shrimp in batches for 2–3 minutes until the noodles are crisp and prawns/shrimp are cooked through.

Turn off the oven and set in the still-warm oven while you cook the remaining prawns/shrimp in the same way.

Serve with the sweet chilli sauce.

Mee grob Thailand

Sometimes called 'mee krob', this crispy noodle dish is one of my favourite Thai starters. Be careful when deep-frying noodles as the oil bubbles up quite dramatically.

100 g/3½ oz. dried rice vermicelli noodles
   (see page 14)
2 eggs, beaten
125 g/1 cup firm tofu, cubed
1 tablespoon dried shrimp (see page 21)
1 Asian shallot (see page 16), thinly sliced
1 tablespoon pickled garlic (see page 157)
50 g/1 cup beansprouts, trimmed
a small bunch of fresh coriander/cilantro
6 garlic chives (see page 18), roughly chopped

vegetable oil, for deep-frying

SAUCE
125 g/½ cup plus 1 tablespoon grated palm sugar
   (see pages 20–21)
1 tablespoon yellow bean sauce (see page 157)
2 tablespoons fish sauce
1 tablespoon freshly squeezed lime juice

Serves 4

Put the noodles in a bowl, cover with boiling water and soak for 20 minutes until softened. Drain the noodles and pat dry with paper towels.

Next make the sauce. Put the palm sugar in a saucepan with 1 tablespoon cold water set over a low heat. Heat gently, stirring continuously, until the sugar dissolves. Turn up the heat and boil for a minute until the syrup turns lightly golden, then stir in the yellow bean paste, fish sauce and lime juice. Simmer gently for 3–4 minutes until thick and keep warm until ready to use.

Pour vegetable oil into a wok or large saucepan to reach about 5 cm/2 in. up the side and set over a medium–high heat. Heat until a cube of bread dropped into the oil crisps in 30 seconds. Add the noodles in small bunches and fry for 1–2 minutes until crisp and golden. Remove with a slotted spoon and drain on paper towels. Repeat with the remaining noodles until you have fried them all. Keep the pan on the heat.

Break the noodles into a large mixing bowl and set aside.

Strain the beaten egg through a fine mesh sieve/strainer and pour half into the hot oil – it will puff up into a lacy cake. Fry for 30 seconds, flip over and fry for a further 30 seconds until crisp and brown, then remove with a slotted spoon. Drain on paper towels and repeat with the remaining egg.

Deep-fry the tofu and set aside.

Deep-fry the dried shrimp for 10 seconds and remove with a slotted spoon.

Carefully discard all but 1 tablespoon of the oil and stir-fry the shallot and garlic for 5 minutes until lightly crisp. Stir in the beansprouts and remove the pan from the heat. Add all the fried ingredients along with the coriander/cilantro and garlic chives to the noodles and stir to combine. Pour in the sauce, stir again and serve at once.

Vegetarian spring rolls Asia

I remember over 30 years ago being introduced to what was then, in the UK, an exotic dish! Back then, going out for a Chinese meal was almost impossible in rural England and it wasn't until I got to London that I discovered a new culinary world. I'll never forget my first spring roll, I was smitten and it marked the beginning of a great love affair with Asian food.

15 g/²⁄₃ cup dried black cloud ear fungus (see page 156)

25 g/1 oz. cellophane noodles (see page 14)

75 g/3 oz. carrots

50 g/a small handful of mangetout/snow peas

1 tablespoon vegetable oil

1 teaspoon freshly grated ginger

25 g/scant ½ cup spinach, torn

1 tablespoon light or dark soy sauce

1 tablespoon oyster sauce

a pinch of freshly ground black pepper

16 large spring roll wrappers (see page 157)

1–2 eggs, lightly beaten

sweet chilli/chile sauce, to serve

a baking sheet lined with baking parchment

Serves 4

Put the mushrooms in a large mixing bowl, cover with boiling water and soak for 20 minutes until softened. Drain well, pat dry with paper towels and slice thinly, discarding any tough stalks. Set aside.

Meanwhile put the noodles in a bowl, cover with boiling water and soak for 30 minutes until softened. Drain the noodles and pat dry with paper towels. Using scissors, cut the noodles into 5 cm/2 in. lengths and set aside.

Cut the carrots into 5-cm/2-in. batons and the mangetout/snow peas into similar-sized shreds.

Heat the oil in a wok or large frying pan/skillet and stir-fry the ginger for a few seconds before adding the carrots and mangetout/snow peas. Stir-fry for 2 minutes before adding the mushrooms, spinach, soy sauce, oyster sauce and black pepper. Stir well and remove the pan from the heat. Stir in the noodles and set aside to cool completely.

Working one wrapper at a time, trim each to 12 x 18 cm/4¾ x 7 in., lay out flat and brush the top with beaten egg. Place a tablespoon of the cooled filling in a log shape along 1 edge of the wrapper. Roll over once, then fold the ends in and over the roll. Continue to roll up tightly to form a sealed parcel.

Preheat the oven to 110°C (225°F) Gas ¼, or the lowest heat setting.

Pour vegetable oil into a wok or large saucepan to reach about 5 cm/2 in. up the side and set over a medium–high heat. Heat until a cube of bread dropped into the oil crisps in 30 seconds. Deep-fry the rolls a few at a time for 1–2 minutes until crisp and golden. Drain on paper towels and transfer the rolls to the prepared baking sheet. Turn off the oven and set in the still-warm oven while you cook the remaining rolls in the same way.

Serve the spring rolls hot with sweet chilli/chile sauce.

noodle soups

Noodle soups

Soup is one of our most comforting dishes and I am a firm believer in scoffing down a bowl of chicken soup when I'm feeling under the weather. It's not just an old wives' tale, either – the nutritious content of a stock made from a chicken carcass is antimicrobial and, in turn, good for you (see Chicken noodle soup, page 72). Soups are nurturing and noodle soups even more so – it's that slurp thing again. In fact in the East soups are consumed as much for their health benefits as their flavour and in Chinese culture soups are closely linked with theories of traditional medicine and often include medicinal herbs.

I talked a little about a good stock in the Noodle basics chapter and nowhere is a good stock more important than in creating a delicious soup. I decided to give only two stock recipes as Asian soups tend to be made with Chicken stock (see page 25) rather than beef or fish, while in Japan it is Dashi broth (see page 25) that plays a more predominant role. Noodles too will vary according to the type of soup. Delicate cellophane, rice vermicelli or somen noodles (see pages 12–15) are used in thinner, often clear broths. Wheat and egg noodles (see pages 12–13) are more robust and are better in thicker, more substantial broths, and then coconut soups and stew-like dishes tend to include thicker rice sticks or flat, wide noodles (see pages 14–15).

Across Asia it is quite normal to serve soups as a breakfast dish – something that we in the West find strange – but if you've ever had one you'll know just how good it can be to start the day with an invigorating bowl of noodle soup. Travel through Thailand, Vietnam, Laos or Cambodia and you'll no doubt come across a floating market where tiny hawker boats sell soup straight from the pot into a bowl as they pass by. In Myanmar, Mohinga (see page 96) is thought by many to be Myanmar's national dish and is served from breakfast through to early afternoon. It is thickened with chickpea/gram flour, producing something akin to a French potage.

During my first ever trip to Asia I travelled to the Cameron Highlands, Malaysia's tea-growing region north of Kuala Lumpar, to spend what turned out to be an uncharacteristically cool and damp Christmas Day in a weird tourist hotel where fake Christmas trees filled the foyer and piped carols played relentlessly on a loop. Thankfully en route, in torrential rain, we stopped at a small row of shops where in the middle sat a tiny, unassuming restaurant. Although basic, the place was packed with locals all eating the same meal. In the centre of the table was a weird-looking cooking pot I'd never seen before with a funnel in the centre and a portable stove underneath – 'Ah,' I thought, 'the Malaysian answer to fondue.' I couldn't have been more wrong or more pleasantly surprised.

This was of course an Asian steamboat where a stock is set to simmer surrounded by an endless supply of seafood, vegetables, herbs, chillies/chiles, condiments and of course noodles. The idea is the same as a fondue, where you cook your own food in the stock, adding depth to the flavour as you go. That's really where the similarity ends – it's a terrific way of eating freshly cooked ingredients but most of all it adds to the sense of sharing and community that abounds everywhere in Asia. I have included a very simplified version of the steamboat we enjoyed that day (see page 87) as you can go to town here making a real feast.

With Japanese soups, it is ramen that fascinate me. Although often associated with fast or instant noodles, the word 'ramen' describes both a type of noodle and the soup itself. So revered in Japan it even spawned the highly entertaining noodle western Tampopo, where the heroine must out-ramen the baddies! At its core a ramen is made with a good fatty broth (which in an ideal world would take days to prepare), plenty of noodles – thick, thin or otherwise and then a range of toppings from chashu (braised pork), eggs, bamboo shoots, various root vegetables and spring onions/scallions. I give a much simplified recipe in the book, Shio ramen (see page 79), but hopefully it will give you a taste of what this soup is about.

If you are ever in New York City, check out Ivan Ramen Slurp Shop – chef Ivan Orkin knows a thing or two about a good ramen.

Soups in Asia tend to be simple, taking little time to prepare and cook and many of these are fresh, clean-tasting clear broths that invigorate the senses. They are healthy and varied and regularly served as a complete meal rather than one course within a larger one. In Vietnamese and Thai cooking the emphasis is on fast, fresh and fiery flavours and the soups are often little more than stock, fresh herbs and aromatics with rice noodles to add bulk while others like the classic Vietnamese Beef pho, pronounced 'fuh' (see page 91) take longer with a richly flavoured beef stock. Chinese soups are made with egg noodles that tend to be more comforting and wonton soups are commonplace. Japanese soups range from straightforward noodles in a clear broth to tempura seafood noodles like the Ramen with tempura prawns/shrimp on page 80, and those with complex stocks and many different stages that take several days to make. Then there are the soups enriched with coconut milk from parts of Thailand, Malaysia and Singapore.

Throughout the following pages you will find a balance of different types of soups. Many will provide a meal in themselves such as Spicy noodle seafood broth (see page 75)or Malaysian Chicken laksa (see page 84) while others make the perfect starter/appetizer or light lunch, try the Mushroom udon (see page 76) or perhaps the Prawn, pea, peashoot and noodle soup (see page 88). Some will include fish and seafood that might be hard to find, but don't be put off just replace my suggestions with what you can buy. It is worth noting that many Asian supermarkets stock a fabulous and quite incredible range of frozen seafood and this is generally of a really high standard.

When adding noodles to any soup it is important to eat the soup as soon as you can, as hot as you can. If left to sit, noodles absorb liquid like a sponge, they lose their texture and the soup loses its stock! Whatever you decide, don't forget to slurp.

Chicken noodle soup China

It's no wonder chicken soup is known for its soothing medicinal properties as well as its flavour – it tastes so good and so healthy with an underlying hint of ginger and garlic from the stock. This is a simple soup, but with a really good stock as a base it's hard to beat.

200 g/7 oz. dried Hokkein noodles (see page 13)
1.25 litres/2 pints Chicken stock (see page 25)
2 teaspoons freshly grated ginger
2 tablespoons light soy sauce
2 tablespoons shaoxing rice wine (see page 20)
1 tablespoon oyster sauce
200 g/1½ cups sliced chicken breast fillet
250 g/about 6 whole pak choi/bok choy, trimmed and roughly chopped
2 spring onions/scallions, trimmed and thinly sliced, plus extra to serve
salt, to taste

GARNISHES (OPTIONAL)
fresh chillies/chiles, sliced
a small bunch of fresh coriander/cilantro

Serves 4

Plunge the noodles into a saucepan of boiling water and cook for 3–4 minutes until al dente. Drain, refresh under cold water and shake dry. Set aside.

Pour the stock into a large saucepan with the ginger, soy sauce, rice wine and oyster sauce and set over a medium heat. Bring slowly to the boil, then simmer for 5 minutes.

Stir in the chicken, pak choi/bok choy and spring onions/scallions and simmer for 3–4 minutes until the chicken is cooked.

Divide the noodles between bowls, pour over the chicken soup and serve with some sliced chillies/chiles and fresh coriander/cilantro, if using.

TIP: If using fresh Hokkein noodles cook for 2 minutes instead of 3–4. If using vacuum-packed, pre-cooked noodles rinse under boiling water only before use. For either you will need 500 g/1 lb.

Spicy noodle seafood broth Korea

This richly flavoured soup is hot and spicy so feel free to temper the heat to your tastes and perhaps bear in mind that most traditional recipes ask for four or five times the amount of spice than I use. I like to serve it with extra gochujang (Korean chilli sauce) on the side for guests to alter the heat of the broth themselves.

200 g/7 oz. dried udon noodles
  (see page 12)
2 tablespoons vegetable oil
2.5 cm/1 in. fresh ginger, peeled and thinly
  sliced
150 g/1 cup sliced pork fillet
2 spring onions/scallions, trimmed and
  cut into batons
2–3 teaspoons gochujang (see page 156),
  plus extra to serve
3 tablespoons dark soy sauce

1 large carrot, cut into batons
1 courgette/zucchini, cut into batons
100 g/1¾ cups sliced white cabbage
100 g/2 cups shiitake mushrooms, stalks
  trimmed and halved
1.5 litres/2½ pints Chicken stock
  (see page 25)
24 small clams
20 prawns/shrimp
200 g/7 oz. cleaned squid bodies

Serves 4

Plunge the noodles into a saucepan of boiling water and cook for about 4 minutes or until al dente. Drain, refresh under cold water and shake dry. Set aside.

Heat the oil in a wok or large frying pan/skillet set over a high heat and stir-fry the ginger for 10 seconds. Add the pork and stir-fry for 2–3 minutes until browned. Add the spring onions/scallions, gochujang and soy sauce and fry for a further 2–3 minutes.

Add the vegetables, stir well, then stir in the stock. Simmer gently for 10 minutes until the vegetables are al dente.

Meanwhile prepare the seafood. Wash and dry the clams, shell and de-vein the prawns/shrimp and cut along one side of the squid bodies to open out, insides up. Using a sharp knife, score a diamond pattern over the squid and cut into large pieces.

Add the seafood to the pan and cook gently until the clams have opened and the prawns and squid are cooked.

Add the noodles to warm through and serve at once.

Mushroom udon _Japan_

This is a light, delicately flavoured mushroom soup. Vegetarians may want to make a version of dashi without the bonito flakes – see page 21 for alternatives. You should be able to buy most of the mushrooms fairly readily from larger supermarkets or online, but could substitute like for like with mushrooms you are able to find.

200 g/7 oz. dried udon noodles
1.5 litres/2½ pints Dashi broth (see
   page 25)
50 ml/scant ¼ cup dark soy sauce
3 tablespoons mirin
2 tablespoons sake
500 g/1 lb. mixed mushrooms,
   including shiitake, oyster and enoki
150 g/1 cup sugar snap peas, trimmed

and cut in half lengthways
200 g/2 cups cubed silken/soft tofu
   (see page 157)
2 tablespoons dried wakame seaweed
   (see page 20)
seven-spice powder (see page 157),
   to serve

Serves 4

Plunge the noodles into a saucepan of boiling water and cook for 4–5 minutes or until al dente. Drain, refresh under cold water and shake dry. Set aside.

Pour the broth, soy sauce, mirin and sake into a saucepan set over a medium heat and bring to the boil. Add the mushrooms except the enoki and simmer gently for 5 minutes until the mushrooms are tender. Stir in the sugar snap peas and enoki mushrooms and simmer for 2 minutes.

Divide the noodles between warmed bowls and top with the tofu and seaweed, pour over the soup and serve at once, sprinkled with seven-spice powder.

Shio Ramen with pork and eggs Japan

Every now and then a cookbook comes along that spends weeks next to my bed so I can read it nightly, absorbing the recipes to use at a later date. This happened with a book called 'Ivan Ramen', by an American ramen aficionado. The story is fascinating and the recipes inspirational. This is inspired by one such recipe, albeit a shorter version.

1 tablespoon sake
1 tablespoon mirin
1 garlic clove, crushed
1 teaspoon freshly
  grated ginger
50 ml/¼ cup dark soy
  sauce
50 ml/¼ cup light soy
  sauce
1 tablespoon caster/
  granulated sugar
750 g/1½ lb. piece of
  pork belly, skin
  removed
4 eggs
2 litres/3½ pints
  Chicken stock (see
  page 25)
250 g/9 oz. dried ramen
  noodles (see page 12)
spring onions/scallions,
  thinly sliced to
  garnish

Serves 4

Pour the sake and mirin into a small saucepan set over a medium heat and bring slowly to the boil. Add the garlic, ginger, dark and light soy sauces and the sugar, and stir until the sugar dissolves. Bring to the boil and simmer very gently for 5 minutes. Remove from the heat and leave to cool.

Cut the pork belly in half across the grain to make two similar squares and put in a saucepan into which the pork fits snugly.

Pour over the cooled soy mixture, return to the heat and bring to the boil. Cover and simmer gently for 1 hour or until the pork is tender. Remove the pan from the heat but leave the pork in the stock to cool at room temperature. Remove the pork from the stock, reserving the stock, and cut into thick slices. Set aside.

Put the eggs in a saucepan of cold water and set over a high heat. Bring to the boil and simmer for 5 minutes. Remove the eggs from the pan and immediately rinse under cold running water until they are cool enough to handle. Peel the eggs and place them in a clean bowl. Pour over the reserved pork stock and leave to soak for 30 minutes. Lift the eggs from the stock and cut in half lengthways.

Meanwhile bring the chicken stock to the boil in a large saucepan and simmer until reduced by about one-third to 1.25 litres/2 pints. Remove from the heat and stir in 4 tablespoons of the reserved pork stock. Add the pork belly slices and warm through for 5 minutes.

Plunge the noodles into a saucepan of boiling water, return to the boil and cook for about 4 minutes or until al dente. Drain well, then divide the noodles between soup bowls. Spoon over the stock and pork slices, add 2 egg halves to each bowl and serve garnished with spring onions/scallions.

Ramen with tempura prawns Japan

Like all Japanese dishes it is the contrast of textures and flavours that defines this dish. The soft slurp of noodles is balanced with the crisp tempura batter which, once submerged into the hot stock, becomes soft, gooey and comforting to eat.

8 large prawns/shrimp
1.5 litres/2½ pints Dashi
    broth (see page 25)
125 ml/½ cup Japanese
    soy sauce
75 ml/scant ⅓ cup mirin
250 g/9 oz. dried ramen
    noodles (see page 12)
125 g/2 handfuls
    mangetout/snow peas,
    trimmed and thinly
    sliced
2 tablespoons dried
    wakame seaweed (see
    page 20)
150 g/1 cup plus 1
    tablespoon cubed firm
    tofu
2 large spring onions/
    scallions, trimmed and
    thinly sliced
vegetable oil, for deep-
    frying

TEMPURA BATTER
1 egg yolk
250 ml/1 cup iced water
100 g/¾ cup plain/all-
    purpose flour
2 tablespoons potato (or
    rice) flour (see page 157)

Serves 4

Peel the prawns/shrimp, leaving the tail section intact and reserving the shells and head. Cut down the back of each one and pull out the black intestinal tract. Wash and dry the prawns/shrimp and set aside. Put the shells and heads in a saucepan set over a medium heat and pour in the broth. Bring to the boil, cover and simmer for 30 minutes. Strain through a fine mesh sieve/strainer and return the stock to the pan. Add the soy sauce and mirin and set aside.

Plunge the noodles into a saucepan of boiling water and cook for about 4 minutes, or until al dente. Drain, refresh under cold water and shake dry. Set aside.

To make the tempura batter, put the egg yolk, iced water and both flours in a large mixing bowl. Very lightly beat the mixture together using a fork to make a slightly lumpy but thin batter.

Return the broth mixture to a simmer, add the mangetout/snow peas and seaweed and simmer for 2 minutes. Add the noodles and cook for 1 minute to heat through.

Meanwhile heat about 5 cm/2 in. of oil in a wok or old saucepan until a cube of bread dropped into the oil crisps and turns brown in 20–30 seconds. Dip the prawns/shrimp into the tempura batter, shaking off any excess. Fry in batches for 2–3 minutes until crisp and golden. Carefully remove the cooked prawns/shrimp and drain on paper towels. Add a little of the remaining tempura batter to the oil and cook until crisp. Drain this and put with the prawns/shrimp.

Divide the noodles between warmed soup bowls, add the tofu and spring onions/scallions, then pour over the soup. Top each with two tempura prawns/shrimp and sprinkle the crispy batter bits into the soup. Serve at once.

Dimsum duck wonton soup Singapore

This recipe is adapted from several dishes I have enjoyed in many different Chinese restaurants around the world. Despite the fact that Chinese BBQ duck is somewhat clichéd, that doesn't stop it from being absolutely delicious if done well, of course. Here, to add a little fun to this soup, the duck, spring onions/scallions, cucumber and hoisin sauce form the filling for wontons. And the skin is deep fried to add a fabulous bite to the finished soup.

½ cooked Chinese BBQ duck
1 small onion, roughly chopped
5 cm/2 in. fresh ginger, peeled, sliced and pounded
4 garlic cloves
3 whole star anise, lightly bruised
1 cinnamon stick, lightly bruised
75 ml/scant ⅓ cup shaoxing rice wine (see page 20)
75 ml/scant ⅓ cup dark soy sauce
½ cucumber, deseeded and finely chopped
2 large spring onions/ scallions, trimmed and finely chopped
2 tablespoons hoisin sauce
1 egg, beaten
24 wonton wrappers (see page 157)
vegetable oil, for deep frying
2 pak choi/bok choy, trimmed and thickly sliced
1 tablespoon chopped fresh coriander/cilantro

TO SERVE
crispy duck skin
coriander/cilantro leaves

Remove the skin and meat from the duck and place the bones in a saucepan with 2 litres/3½ pints of cold water. Add the onion, ginger, garlic, star anise and cinnamon stick and bring to the boil over a medium heat. Partially cover the pan and simmer gently for 30 minutes. Strain the stock through a fine mesh sieve/strainer into a clean saucepan and stir in the shaoxing and soy sauce.

Meanwhile, chop the duck meat and put in a bowl with the cucumber, spring onions/scallions and hoisin sauce. Add half the beaten egg and mix to combine.

Working one at a time, lay the wonton wrappers out flat and place a tablespoon of the duck filling in the middle of each. Brush the edges with the remaining beaten egg and press together to seal.

Heat about 5 cm/2 in. oil in a wok or old saucepan until a cube of bread dropped into the oil crisps and turns brown in 20–30 seconds. Cut the duck skin into thin strips and fry in the hot oil until crispy. Remove from the pan and drain on paper towels.

Bring the duck stock to a gentle simmer, add the wontons and cook for 5 minutes. Remove with a slotted spoon and divide between serving bowls. Add the pak choi/bok choy to the stock and simmer for 2–3 minutes until tender. Divide the pak choi/bok choy between the bowls and pour over the stock.

Serve the soup with the crispy duck skin and a few coriander/cilantro leaves sprinkled on top.

Serves 4

250 g/9 oz. dried rice stick
  noodles (see page 14)
2 large skinless chicken breast
  fillets (about 350 g/12 oz.)
1 litre/1¾ pints Chicken stock
  (see page 25)
2 tablespoons vegetable oil
400 ml/1⅔ cups coconut milk
200 ml/¾ cup coconut cream
2 tablespoons fish sauce
2 teaspoons caster/granulated
  sugar

LAKSA PASTE
6 shallots, chopped
4 garlic cloves, chopped
2 lemon grass stalks, thinly
  sliced
2 large red bird's eye chillies/
  chiles, deseeded and sliced
2.5 cm/1 in. fresh galangal
  (see page 19), peeled and
  chopped
2.5 cm/1 in. fresh turmeric,
  peeled and chopped (or 1
  teaspoon ground turmeric)
4 macadamia nuts
1 tablespoon shrimp paste (see
  page 21)
2 teaspoons coriander seeds,
  toasted and ground

TO SERVE
beansprouts, trimmed
½ cucumber, sliced
deep-fried puffed tofu (see
  page 16)
Deep-fried shallots (see page
  29)
fresh coriander/cilantro or
  Vietnamese mint
1 lime, cut into wedges
Sambal olek (see page 38) or
  Chilli oil (see page 22)

Serves 4

Chicken laksa Malaysia

Laksa is a spicy noodle soup made with coconut milk and either seafood, pork or chicken. It is always adorned with a selection of garnishes. Malaysian food draws on its rich heritage of cultures from Chinese to Indian and these combine here with the use of spices, herbs and coconut to create a truly unique soup.

Soak the noodles in a bowlful of hot water for 20–30 minutes until softened. Drain well, shake dry and set aside.

Put the chicken breast in a saucepan with the stock set over a low–medium heat. Simmer very gently for 10 minutes until the chicken is just cooked. Remove the chicken from the stock and set aside to cool completely. Once cool, slice thinly.

To make the laksa paste, pound all the ingredients together in a large pestle and mortar or blitz in a food processor until smooth.

Heat the oil in a wok or non-stick saucepan set over a medium heat and add the laksa paste. Fry for 2 minutes until fragrant, then add the coconut milk and chicken stock. Simmer gently for 10 minutes and then stir in the coconut cream, fish sauce and sugar. Simmer gently for a further 2–3 minutes.

Divide the noodles between bowls and add the sliced chicken. Pour over the hot soup and serve topped with a selection of garnishes. Pass around a pot of sambal olek or chilli oil, to drizzle.

Seafood steamboat Malaysia

Most Asian countries make some sort of large seafood hotpot and Malaysia is no different.
This is based on my first-ever experience of this wonderful dish.

350 g/11½ oz. dried rice
  vermicelli noodles (see page
  14)
2 litres/3½ pints Chicken
  stock (see page 25)
4 tablespoons fish sauce
2 tablespoons grated palm
  sugar (see pages 20–21)
250 g/9 oz. skinless white fish
  fillets, such as cod, ling or
  pollock
250 g/9 oz. cleaned squid
  bodies
250 g/3¾ cups (about 25)
  medium prawns/shrimp
250 g/about 15 scallops
250 g/9 oz. (about 25) fresh
  clams (or about 10 mussels),
  cleaned
125 g/1½ cups choi sum (see
  page 16)

TO SERVE
a handful each of fresh Thai
  basil, mint and coriander/
  cilantro
red chillies/chiles, sliced
2 limes, cut into wedges

Serves 6

Soak the noodles in a bowlful of hot water for 10–20 minutes until softened.
Drain well, shake dry and set aside.

Pour the stock into a large saucepan set over a medium heat. Add the fish sauce
and sugar and bring to the boil. Once boiling, reduce the heat but keep warm.

Next prepare the seafood. Remove any bones from the fish and cut into
2.5-cm/1-in. cubes. Open out the squid body by cutting down one side and
score the inside flesh with a sharp knife in a diamond pattern. Cut into
2.5-cm/1-in. pieces.

Peel the prawns/shrimp, leaving the tail section intact. Cut down the back
of each one almost in half and pull out the black intestinal tract. Wash and dry
the prawns/shrimp and set aside.

Trim the grey muscle from the side of each scallop and set aside.

Arrange all the seafood, cooked noodles and the choi sum on a large platter
on the table.

Place a portable gas burner in the middle of the table and pour half the
chicken stock into a smaller saucepan. Bring to a gentle simmer (keeping the
remaining stock warm on the stove). Place the bowls of garnishes next to each
guest along with a serving bowl and noodles.

Using tongs, the guests can then cook the seafood and choi sum in the hot
stock, which will become increasingly flavoursome. As the food cooks, spoon
it into the serving bowls with some noodles and a little of the stock and top with
fresh herbs, chillies/chiles and lime juice. Top up with more stock as required.

Prawn, pea and pea shoot soup *Vietnam*

Near to my home in London in the 1990s, the Vietnamese Canteen opened in what was a very residential street. It was unassuming, basic, run by Vietnamese people and packed. This is based on my favourite soup they served there.

350 g/12 oz. dried rice stick noodles (see page 14)
1.25 litres/2 pints Chicken stock (see page 25)
1 small onion, sliced
4 garlic cloves, roughly chopped
2 red bird's eye chillies/chiles, pounded
6 kaffir lime leaves (see page 156), pounded
2.5 cm/1 in. galangal (see page 19), sliced and bruised
2 lemon grass stalks, trimmed and bruised
3 tablespoons fish sauce
2 tablespoons freshly squeezed lime juice

1 tablespoon grated palm sugar (see pages 20–21)
2 celery sticks, sliced
2 tomatoes, peeled, deseeded and diced
500 g/7½ cups (about 50) medium prawns/shrimp, peeled and de-veined
150 g/3 cups peas
a handful of pea shoots
a handful of fresh herbs, such as perilla leaves (see page 18) and coriander/cilantro

Serves 4

Soak the noodles in a bowlful of hot water for 20–30 minutes until softened. Drain well, shake dry and set aside.

Put the stock, onion, garlic, chillies/chiles, lime leaves, galangal and lemon grass in a saucepan set over a medium heat and bring to the boil. Simmer gently for 10 minutes until the soup is fragrant, then strain the stock through a fine mesh sieve/strainer into a clean saucepan.

Stir in the fish sauce, lime juice and sugar, and set over a medium heat. Add the celery and tomatoes and simmer for 5 minutes. Add the prawns/shrimp and peas, and simmer for a further 2–3 minutes, until the prawns/shrimp are just cooked through.

Divide the noodles between bowls and pour over the soup. Serve topped with pea shoots and herbs.

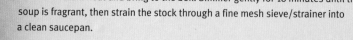

Beef pho Vietnam

Whenever I visit a city with a Vietnamese population I always try and make a trip to wherever the majority of Vietnamese have settled so I can treat myself to an authentic beef pho. It's the large baskets of colourful herbs and condiments that give this classic soup its freshness and that unique flavour and texture I love so much. To allow the flavours to develop, you need to prepare this dish a day in advance.

1 kg/2 lb. beef short ribs
5 cm/2 in. fresh ginger, peeled, sliced and pounded
1 onion, sliced
2 garlic cloves, sliced
3 whole star anise, pounded
2 cinnamon sticks, pounded
400 g/14 oz. dried rice stick noodles (see page 14)
350 g/1⅓ cups thinly sliced beef fillet
3 tablespoons fish sauce
1 teaspoon salt
1 teaspoon caster/granulated sugar
freshly squeezed juice of 1 lime
125 g/2⅓ cups bean sprouts, trimmed

GARNISHES
2 red bird's eye chillies/chiles, chopped
a handful each of fresh Thai basil, Vietnamese mint and coriander/cilantro
6 spring onions/scallions, trimmed and sliced

Serves 4

Put the ribs in a large saucepan, cover with cold water and bring to the boil. Simmer for 10 minutes then drain and wash the ribs. Return them to the pan and add 2 litres/3½ cups more cold water along with the ginger, onion, garlic, star anise and cinnamon. Return to the boil and simmer gently for 1½ hours, or until the meat is tender.

Carefully remove the ribs from the stock and set aside to cool. Thinly shred the meat, discarding bones. Strain the stock through a fine mesh sieve/strainer and set aside to cool. Refrigerate both the meat and the stock overnight.

The next day, soak the noodles in a bowlful of hot water for 20–30 minutes, until softened. Drain well, shake dry and divide the noodles between large bowls.

Meanwhile, skim and discard the layer of fat from the cold stock and return the pan to a medium heat until just boiling. Stir in the shredded meat, beef fillet, fish sauce, salt, sugar and lime juice. Place the beef fillet on the noodles, spoon over the stock and top with the beansprouts.

Serve with a plate of the garnishes in the middle of the table for everyone to help themselves.

Hot and sour fish soup Laos

Unlike those of its neighbours, Laotian cuisine tends to be sour and salty rather than sweet, sour and salty like this one. The addition of the roasted tomato salsa adds a fiery heat to the soup and a light smokey flavour. This would traditionally be made with river fish such as catfish or carp but you can use whatever fish you like.

200 g/9 oz. cellophane noodles (see page 14)
6 kaffir lime leaves (see page 156), torn
1 large red chilli/chile, roughly chopped
2.5 cm/1 in. fresh ginger, peeled and chopped
1 lemon grass stalk, trimmed and roughly chopped
2 garlic cloves
1.5 litres/2½ pints Chicken stock (see page 25)
2 shallots, finely chopped

500 g/1 lb. fish steaks or fillets, such as striped bass or bream
50 g/1 cup spinach, torn
4 tablespoons Jeow marg leng (see page 41), plus extra to serve
freshly squeezed juice of 1 lime
2 tablespoons fish sauce
a bunch of fresh coriander/cilantro

Serves 4

Soak the noodles in a bowlful of hot water for 10 minutes until softened. Drain well, shake dry and set aside.

Put the lime leaves, chilli/chile, ginger, lemon grass and garlic in a pestle and mortar and pound together until fragrant – it should still be quite bitty. Transfer this paste to a saucepan set over a medium heat and pour over the stock. Bring to the boil then simmer gently for 20 minutes until really fragrant.

Add the shallots and simmer for 5 minutes, then carefully add the fish fillets and cook gently for 4–5 minutes until cooked through. Remove the pan from the heat and stir in the spinach, jeow marg leng, lime juice, fish sauce and coriander/cilantro. Cover with a lid and set aside for 5 minutes to allow the flavours to develop.

Divide the noodles between bowls and carefully spoon the fish on top, pour over the soup and serve at once with extra jeow marg leng.

Vermicelli soup with river fish — Laos

Being landlocked, Laos makes best use of its many rivers and the fish that thrive there. This is typical of the type of fish soup that is eaten daily in Laos. Traditionally, the stock would be flavoured with a ham hock, the meat being added to the soup, but I tend to use a smoked gammon knuckle for a wonderfully smokey flavour.

4 Asian shallots (see page 16), halved
4 garlic cloves (skin on)
4 large red chillies/chiles
1 kg/2 lb. smoked gammon knuckle
5 cm/2 in. fresh galangal, peeled and sliced
6 kaffir limes leaves (see page 156), pounded
2 tablespoons fish sauce
250 g/9 oz. dried rice vermicelli (see page 14)
100 g/½ small green papaya, peeled and shredded
50 g/⅓ cup drained and sliced bamboo shoots (optional)
125 g/¼ Chinese cabbage, thinly sliced
50 g/5–6 snake beans (see page 16), trimmed and thinly sliced
250 g/9 oz. river fish fillets, such as trout or perch

TO SERVE
2 limes, cut into wedges
fresh chillies/chiles, chopped
fresh Thai basil leaves

Serves 4–6

Preheat a stovetop ridged grill pan over a medium heat until it's smoking hot. Arrange the shallots cut-side down in the pan along with the garlic cloves and chillies/chiles. Char-grill for 5 minutes, turn over and cook for a further 5 minutes until everything is well charred.

Place the gammon in a large saucepan with 3 litres/5¼ pints of cold water, the charred vegetables, the galangal, kaffir lime leaves and fish sauce. Set over a high heat and bring to the boil. Simmer gently for 1½ hours, skimming any scum from the surface. Carefully remove the gammon, discard the skin and cut the meat into shreds. Set aside.

Soak the noodles in a bowlful of hot water for 20 minutes until softened. Drain well and arrange on a platter with the papaya, bamboo shoots, cabbage and snake beans.

Return the shredded meat to the stock and add the fish, simmer gently for 2–3 minutes until the fish is cooked. Stir in the noodles and sliced snake beans.

Serve the soup from the pan so everyone can help themselves to the noodles, vegetables, herbs and other garnishes.

Mohinga Myanmar

200 g/7 oz. dried rice
  vermicelli noodles (see page
  14)
1 lemon grass stalk, trimmed
  and finely chopped
2 garlic cloves, roughly
  chopped
2 teaspoons freshly grated
  ginger
1 teaspoon shrimp paste (see
  page 21)
1 tablespoon fish sauce
3 tablespoons vegetable oil
1 onion, thinly sliced
50 g/2 oz. banana stem or
  canned palm heart (see page
  156), sliced (optional)
1 teaspoon ground turmeric
¼ teaspoon dried red chilli/
  hot red pepper flakes
250 g/9 oz. skinless white fish
  fillet, finely chopped or
  minced
1.25 litres/2 pints Chicken
  stock (see page 25)
40 g/½ cup chickpea/gram
  flour (see page 156), toasted

GARNISHES
2 hardboiled/hard-cooked
  eggs, peeled and finely
  chopped
2 tablespoons Deep-fried
  shallots (see page 29)
2 tablespoons Sambal olek
  (see page 38)

Serves 4

Burmese food is full of influences from its neighbouring countries and their cultures, but also present are Indian influences like spices and chickpea/gram flour used as a thickening agent. Mohinga is an aromatic noodle soup served mainly for breakfast. In fact Mohinga is considered by many as Myanmar's national dish and is served at hawkers' stalls all over the country.

Soak the noodles in a bowlful of hot water for 10–20 minutes until softened. Drain well, shake dry and set aside.

Grind the lemon grass, garlic, ginger, shrimp paste and fish sauce together in a pestle and mortar or food processor to form a thin paste.

Heat the oil in a saucepan set over a medium heat and gently fry the onion and banana stem, if using (leave the palm hearts until later), for 5 minutes until softened. Stir in the turmeric and chilli/hot red pepper flakes and cook for 1 minute. Add the lemon grass paste and fry for a further 5 minutes.

Add the minced fish and cook, stirring continuously, until golden. Pour in the stock and bring to the boil.

Meanwhile, combine the toasted chickpea/gram flour with 2 tablespoons cold water in a bowl until smooth. Stir in 3–4 tablespoons of the hot stock and then whisk the whole lot back into the soup. Bring to the boil, stirring continuously, and simmer for 5 minutes.

Divide the noodles between serving bowls. Spoon over the soup and serve with a large platter of the garnishes.

Num banh chok *Cambodia*

250 g/9 oz. dried rice stick
noodles (see page 14)
350 g/11 oz. bream or snapper
fillets, cut into 2.5-cm/1-in.
pieces
250 ml/1 cup Chicken stock
(see page 25)
125 ml/½ cup coconut cream
125 ml/½ cup coconut milk
1 tablespoon fish sauce
2 teaspoons grated palm sugar
(see pages 20–21)

LEMON GRASS PASTE
6 lemon grass stalks
2.5 cm/1 in. fresh galangal
(see page 19), peeled and
roughly chopped
2.5 cm/1 in. fresh turmeric,
peeled and roughly chopped
2 kaffir lime leaves (see page
156), shredded
2 garlic cloves, roughly
chopped
2 tablespoons chopped
peanuts
1 teaspoon shrimp paste (see
page 21)
1 teaspoon freshly grated
ginger

TO SERVE
½ cucumber, sliced
60 g/1 cup beansprouts
lotus root (optional, see page
156)

Serves 4

'Khmer noodles' is the generic name given to num banh chok, a classic Cambodian soup traditionally served at breakfast or as an afternoon snack. Although you will find regional differences it is always made with a freshly pounded lemon grass paste, fish, noodles and a selection of crisp raw vegetables and fresh herbs.

Soak the noodles in a bowlful of hot water for 20 minutes until softened. Drain well using a kitchen cloth and set aside.

To make the lemon grass paste, discard the hard end of the lemon grass stalk and peel away and discard the hard outer leaves until you reach the soft core of the stalk. Trim lengths of about 5 cm/2 in. and roughly chop the remaining core. Place the lemon grass in a food processor with the remaining ingredients and blend to a smooth paste.

Heat the oil in a wok or saucepan set over a medium heat until it starts to shimmer. Add the paste and fry for 2–3 minutes until fragrant. Add the fish pieces and fry gently for 2 minutes until cooked. Remove the fish from the pan as carefully as you can and set aside.

Add the stock, coconut cream and coconut milk to the pan and simmer gently for 10 minutes until thick and creamy. Stir in the fish sauce and sugar, and simmer for a final minute.

Divide the noodles between bowls and top with the pieces of fish. Pour over the broth and serve with bowls of sliced cucumber, beansprouts and lotus root.

noodle salads

Noodle salads

Noodles lend themselves perfectly to being used in salads. Once cooked or rehydrated they provide the ideal base for a whole range of fresh vegetables, herbs, meats, seafood and dressings. They add a neutral layer to a dish, balancing the fire of the chillies/chiles, the sharpness of lime juice or acidity of the dressing.

Traditionally Asian salads are very simple affairs, just a few ingredients tossed in a simple dressing. They are the perfect balance between sweet and sour, crispy yet tender but above all they are lighter than many Western salads. Perhaps this is due to the dressings, which rarely include oil, something that makes them healthier as well. Dressings invariably include a sweet element – usually palm sugar balanced with the saltiness of fish sauce or soy sauce and the necessary tartness provided by lime juice or rice vinegar. Texture is added with crunchy toppings such as Deep-fried shallots (see page 29), toasted chopped nuts or toasted ground rice (see page 157). Both meat and seafood are included but rarely in large amounts. In fact, I often find the beauty of Asian salads is their simplicity.

Asian salads are rarely served as a single course, but do play an important part in everyday meals being served alongside other dishes, once again providing a balance so important in the culture of Asian cuisines. So with a hot and spicy curry you might expect to find a cooler, refreshing plate of shredded cucumber or grated vegetables. It is less common to find many actual noodle salads but rather cooled noodles served with a selection of char-grilled meat or fish, raw vegetables, lettuce leaves and an abundance of fresh herbs.

Of course there are some wonderful Asian main course/entrée salads, typically in Thai and Laotian dishes but, as a lover of salads, I wanted to include a selection of my favourite combinations, incorporating noodles in traditional ways as well as some more fusion-style recipes.

All types of noodles can be used in salads. Cellophane and rice vermicelli noodles are ideal for tangy Thai and Laotian-style salads such as the Crab and mung bean noodles (see page 116). Chinese egg noodles are a perfect foil for the slightly more robust salad with black cloud ear fungus and tofu (see page 104).

Malaysia opened my eyes to amazing and exotic soups, while the fragrant flavours of Thailand and Vietnam inspired a whole new repertoire of salad dishes. I'll never forget the first time I ate green papaya salad, which was actually in Cabramatta and not Asia. Cabramatta is in Sydney's western suburbs where there is the large Vietnamese population and it's really worth a trip out to this vibrant suburb if you are ever visiting Sydney. We had lunch at a restaurant called the Tan Viet noodle house and I ordered green papaya salad largely because I'd never had it before! It was big 'wow' for me, with its simplicity and lovely dressing and I wanted to see if I could make this work with noodles. You'll find the recipe for Green papaya and crispy pork salad on page 112 where the crispy pork adds an extra depth of flavour as well as a foil for the sharpness of the dressing. Traditionally the pork belly would have been slow-cooked over charcoal but I have simplified it and used smoked pancetta.

No doubt one of my other favourite Asian salads is adapted from one I have enjoyed at Longrain, which was something of an institution in the Sydney food scene that possibly served some of the greatest Thai and South-east Asian food outside of Asia itself. This restaurant opened back in 1998 and, although its Sydney branch is currently closed, the Longrain name continues in two extremely popular restaurants, based in Melbourne and Tokyo. The long communal tables mean the restaurant has the energy and buzz that so well defines its food but the standout attraction is still the food itself. This is typified by the Smoked trout, noodle and chilli caramel salad and I've included my interpretation of the recipe in this chapter (see page 119). In my view it's the dressing that transforms this dish into something really special – a caramelized palm sugar sauce infused with chilli/chile heat and the warm and aromatic spicing of cinnamon and star anise. This is used to sweeten and balance the salty tangy of lime juice and fish sauce.

With traditional Chinese dishes, you will rarely come across raw ingredients so salads as we know them are rare but rather we in the West use classic Chinese ingredients to make some fabulous salads that are more suited to our way of eating. It is reported that Chinese chicken salad may well have been invented in California 1960s therefore it's interesting and not a little bizarre that today you will be served salads in some parts of China, especially Szechuan province, as part of a pan-Asian fusion of foods.

One of my favourite combinations in this chapter has to be the Warm noodle and tofu salad (see page 124) from Myanmar, where three or four different varieties of noodle are combined with yet more carbohydrate in the form of rice and potatoes plus silken and puffed tofu, all piled into serving bowls with shredded vegetables, fresh herbs and a lovely spicy dressing. It's already a fusion dish in its own right with influences from all over Asia as well as further afield with the inclusion of potatoes. It is unusual but surprisingly light when you consider all those carbs, try it for yourself.

When preparing any salad, fresh is always best so I recommend that you prepare the dressings first, then assemble all the other ingredients and only combine everything just before you plan to plate up. That way you will be able to detect and appreciate all the individual complex flavours and textures as well as enjoying them as a whole.

Egg noodle, black cloud ear fungus and tofu salad China

The black cloud ear fungus mushrooms used here add a delightful crunch to this Chinese-style tofu salad. You can use plain tofu if you prefer, but I love the slight smokiness from marinated tofu. Different flavours of tofu can be found in most large supermarkets or health food stores, so try out a few varieties to see which you like best.

15 g/1 cup dried black cloud ear fungus (see page 156)
200 g/7 oz. fresh egg noodles (see page 13)
½ cucumber, peeled
1 large carrot
150 g/1 cup plus 1 tablespoon marinated tofu (see page 156), thinly sliced
4 spring onions/scallions, trimmed and thinly sliced
100 g/1⅔ cups Chinese cabbage (see page 156), sliced
a small handful each of fresh mint and coriander/cilantro
1 tablespoon sesame seeds, toasted

DRESSING
2 tablespoons light soy sauce
2 tablespoons brown rice vinegar
1 tablespoon caster/granulated sugar
1 teaspoon sesame oil
1 teaspoon Chilli oil (see page 22)

Serves 4

Put the black cloud ear fungus in a large mixing bowl, cover with boiling water and soak for 20 minutes until softened. Drain well, pat dry with paper towels and slice thinly, discarding any tough stalks. Set aside.

Meanwhile, cook the noodles by plunging them into a saucepan of boiling water. Return to the boil and simmer for 2–3 minutes until al dente. Drain and immediately refresh under cold water before draining again. Dry thoroughly using a clean kitchen cloth and set aside.

Cut the cucumber and carrot into thin strips and place in a large mixing bowl. Add the black cloud ear fungus, tofu, spring onions/scallions, cabbage and herbs and toss well.

To make the dressing, whisk all the ingredients together in a small bowl until the sugar is dissolved.

Stir the noodles into the salad, add the dressing and toss well until evenly combined. Serve in bowls, sprinkled with the sesame seeds.

Chilled noodles with egg Korea

Asian or 'nashi' pears are commonly added to Korean sauces but are also delicious when grated into salads. Serve this salad as a light lunch in summer months.

250 g/9 oz. dried soba noodles
   (see page 12)
2 eggs
1 carrot, peeled and trimmed
1 small cucumber, peeled and
   deseeded
1 Asian pear (see page 156),
   peeled and thinly sliced
100 g/1¾ cups beansprouts
a handful each of mizuna
   leaves and perilla leaves
   (optional, see page 18)

TO SERVE
1 quantity Cho-gochujang (see
   page 34)
a pinch of sesame seeds,
   toasted
Quick kimchi (see page 30)

Serves 4

Cook the noodles by plunging them into a large saucepan of boiling water. Return to the boil and cook for 4 minutes until al dente. Drain and immediately refresh under cold water before draining again. Shake to remove any excess water and set aside.

Put the eggs in a saucepan of cold water and set over a high heat. Bring to the boil and simmer for 8 minutes. Remove the eggs from the pan and immediately rinse under cold, running water until they are cool enough to handle. Peel the eggs and place them in a clean bowl.

Cut the carrot and cucumber into thin strips and put in a large mixing bowl.

Add the noodles to the bowl and toss with the pear, beansprouts, and mizuna and perilla leaves, if using. Divide between serving dishes.

Cut the eggs in half and place one half on each salad. Drizzle over a little of the cho-gochujang and sprinkle with the sesame seeds. Serve with kimchi.

Chicken noodle salad with sesame and soy dressing Japan

This summer salad can be made using any Japanese noodles. When researching for this book I came across these black rice noodles, which make a startling contrast to the different vegetables and micro herbs when arranged on the plate. The end result is striking.

250 g/9 oz. dried black rice
　noodles (see page 14)
100 g/about 7 radishes, trimmed
2 carrots, trimmed
125 g/1½ cups mangetout/snow
　peas, trimmed
½ cucumber, deseeded
250 g/1⅔ cups torn cooked
　chicken breast fillet

1 quantity Wafu dressing (see
　page 33)
Japanese micro herbs (see pages
　157)
1 tablespoon black sesame seeds
　(see page 20)

Serves 4

Plunge the noodles into a large saucepan of boiling water. Return to the boil and simmer for 5–6 minutes until al dente. Drain the noodles and immediately refresh under cold water, washing well to remove any remaining starch. Drain again and dry thoroughly on a clean kitchen cloth. Put the noodles in a large mixing bowl and set aside.

Next, prepare the vegetables. Thinly slice the radishes, carrots and mangetout/snow peas. Cut the cucumber into thin strips, like the carrot.

Arrange the cooled noodles in the middle of each serving plate and place the vegetables in groups around them. Add the torn, cooked chicken and drizzle over the dressing. Scatter over the micro herbs and sesame seeds, and serve at once.

Seared salmon and green tea noodle salad Japan

You can use any type of Japanese noodles for this, but I love the flavour and colour of green tea noodles. The deeply sweet flavour of green tea pairs wonderfully with the soft and soothing texture of the salmon.

200 g/7 oz. green tea soba
   noodles (see page 12)
2 teaspoons sesame oil
250 g/9 oz. fresh sashimi
   salmon fillet
a pinch of smoked sea salt (see
   Tip)
3 tablespoons white and dark
   sesame seeds
a handful each of fresh
   coriander/cilantro and
   mixed baby salad leaves
pickled ginger, to serve
   (optional)

DRESSING
2 tablespoons Dashi broth (see
   page 25)
1½ tablespoons rice wine
   vinegar
2 teaspoons light soy sauce
1 teaspoons caster/granulated
   sugar
1 teaspoon sesame oil

Serves 4

Cook the noodles by plunging them into a large saucepan of boiling water. Return to the boil and cook for 4 minutes until al dente. Drain and immediately refresh under cold water before draining again. Shake to remove any excess water and dry with a clean kitchen cloth. Transfer the noodles to a large mixing bowl, add the sesame oil and toss well to coat.

Meanwhile season the salmon with salt and mixed sesame seeds.

Preheat a non-stick frying pan/skillet over a high heat until smoking, add the salmon and cook for 1 minute each side until seared on the outside but still rare inside. Set aside to cool before slicing thinly.

To make the dressing, combine all the ingredients in a bowl and stir to dissolve the sugar.

Arrange the noodles on a large platter and top with the salmon and coriander/cilantro. Drizzle with the dressing and serve with some pickled ginger, if using.

TIP: Flavoured sea salts are all the rage and smoked sea salt is a lovely addition here. However, you can use regular sea salt if you prefer.

Green papaya and crispy pork salad Vietnam

Green papaya salad is one of my favourite Asian dishes and, like many noodle dishes, varies in flavour enormously. But it is always hot, sour, salty and sweet. I love this version, which uses smoked pancetta for added saltiness and texture.

150 g/5 oz. dried rice vermicelli noodles (see page 14)

150 g/5 oz. pancetta, diced

150 g/⅓ green papaya (see page 16), peeled, halved and deseeded

1 cucumber, deseeded and thinly sliced

a small bunch each of fresh Vietnamese mint, coriander/cilantro and Thai basil

125 g/scant 1 cup grape cherry tomatoes, halved or quartered

2 tablespoons fish sauce

2 tablespoons grated palm sugar (see pages 20–21)

2 tablespoons freshly squeezed lime juice

2 red bird's eye chillies/chiles, deseeded and thinly sliced (if desired)

4 tablespoons dry-roasted peanuts, finely chopped

1 tablespoon toasted ground rice (see page 157)

Deep-fried shallots, to serve (see page 29)

Serves 4

Soak the noodles in a bowlful of hot water for 10–20 minutes until softened. Drain well, pat dry with a kitchen cloth and set aside in a large mixing bowl.

Dry-fry the pancetta in a small frying pan/skillet set over high heat until crisp and golden. Set aside to cool.

Thinly slice the papaya and cut into long thin strips or julienne. Add to the noodles with the cucumber, herbs, cherry tomatoes and pancetta.

Whisk together the fish sauce, sugar and lime juice and stir until the sugar is dissolved. Pour over the salad, toss well and divide between plates.

Top with the fresh red chillies/chiles, if using, peanuts and powdered rice, and serve with deep-fried shallots.

Char-grilled prawns with noodle and herb salad Vietnam

Snaking its way through Vietnam, the Mekong Delta is home to the prawn/shrimp farming industry, producing large succulent prawns/shrimp, perfect for grilling over coals on skewers as here.

24 large prawns/shrimp
1 tablespoon light soy sauce
150 g/5½ oz. rice vermicelli noodles (see page 14)
1 teaspoon sesame oil
½ green papaya, peeled and thinly sliced
50 g/1 cup mixed salad leaves
a handful of fresh herbs such as perilla leaves (see page 18), mint, coriander/cilantro and Thai basil
a small handful of mixed micro herbs (see page 157)
2–3 spring onions/scallions, trimmed and sliced
4 tablespoons peanuts, roasted and chopped
4 tablespoons Deep-fried shallots (see page 29)
1 quantity Nuoc cham (see page 37)
a few kaffir lime leaves (see page 156), thinly sliced, to serve
lime wedges, to serve
24 bamboo skewers, soaked in cold water for 30 minutes

Serves 4

Peel the prawns/shrimp, leaving the tail section intact. Cut down the back of each one and pull out the black intestinal tract. Wash and dry the prawns/shrimp and put in a bowl with the soy sauce. Stir well and set aside to marinate for 30 minutes.

Thread each marinated prawn/shrimp onto the soaked bamboo skewers from head to tail.

Soak the noodles in a bowlful of hot water for 20 minutes until softened. Drain and shake well to dry before transferring to a large mixing bowl. Toss the noodles with the sesame oil, then add the shredded papaya, salad leaves, herbs, micro herbs, spring onions/scallions, peanuts and deep-fried shallots.

Preheat a foil-lined stovetop grill pan over a high heat and cook the prawns/shrimp for 2 minutes on each side until charred and cooked through.

Serve the prawns/shrimp on the side of the salad bowls, drizzled with nuoc cham, garnished with shredded lime leaves and a squeeze of fresh lime.

Crab and mung bean noodles Thailand

If possible, use fresh picked crabmeat for this recipe. Many fishmongers sell crabmeat vacuum packed which is perfect but for the more adventurous cook you could, like me, buy a whole cooked crab and pick out the fresh meat yourself.

100 g/3½ oz. dried cellophane
   noodles (see page 14–15)
250 g/½ cup fresh picked crab
   meat
2 Asian shallots (see page 16),
   thinly sliced
1 celery stick, chopped
2 spring onions/scallions,
   trimmed and thinly sliced
1 long red chilli/chile,
   deseeded and chopped
2 tomatoes, peeled, deseeded
   and diced
a few fresh herbs, including
   basil, coriander/cilantro
   and dill
1 tablespoon fish sauce
freshly squeezed juice of 1 lime
toasted ground rice (see page
   157), to garnish (optional)

Serves 4

Soak the noodles in a bowlful of hot water for 10–20 minutes until softened. Drain well, pat dry with a kitchen cloth and set aside in a large mixing bowl.

Put the noodles in a large mixing bowl with the crab meat, shallots, celery sticks, spring onions/scallions, chilli/chile, tomatoes and herbs. Add the fish sauce and lime juice and toss well to coat.

Transfer the mixture to a serving platter and sprinkle over toasted ground rice, if using.

Smoked trout, noodle and chilli caramel salad Thailand

Martin Boetz, chef at Sydney's Longrain restaurant, is a master of Thai cooking and this recipe is inspired by some of his most delicious recipes. Made with a caramel dressing infused with spices and Thai aromatics for sweetness, this noodle salad is lovely paired with the smokey saltiness of the trout.

125 g/4 oz. dried rice stick noodles (see page 14)
200 g/7 oz. hot smoked trout fillet, flaked
3 spring onions/scallions, trimmed and thinly sliced
1 cucumber, peeled, deseeded and cut into batons
1 large red chilli/chile, deseeded and sliced
2 tablespoons each of torn fresh mint and coriander/cilantro
50 g/½ cup roasted and roughly chopped cashew nuts

DRESSING
125 g/½ cup plus 1 tablespoon grated palm sugar (see pages 20–21)
1 small cinnamon stick, lightly pounded
2 whole star anise, lightly pounded
3 tablespoons fish sauce
2–3 tablespoons freshly squeezed lime juice
1 teaspoon light soy sauce
1 bird's eye red chilli/chile, deseeded and chopped

Serves 4

Begin by making the dressing. Put the palm sugar and 75 ml/scant ⅓ cup cold water in a saucepan set over a medium heat and simmer gently until the sugar dissolves. Stir in the cinnamon and star anise, bring to the boil and cook for 5–10 minutes, until syrupy but do not allow to burn. Turn off the heat and carefully add the fish sauce, lime juice and soy sauce (the caramel will spit). Strain the sauce into a bowl through a fine mesh sieve/strainer and stir in the chilli/chile. Set aside to cool.

Meanwhile, soak the noodles in a bowlful of hot water for 20 minutes until softened. Drain well, pat dry with a kitchen cloth and set aside in a large mixing bowl.

Add the smoked trout to the noodles with the spring onions/scallions, cucumber, red chilli/chile and herbs and drizzle over 2–3 tablespoons of the dressing. Toss well and pile onto a platter.

Serve at once, topped with the toasted cashew nuts.

TIP: Store any remaining dressing in a sterilized glass jar with an airtight lid in the fridge for up to 2 weeks.

Kaffir lime, squid and noodle salad Cambodia

This dish can be found in many guises originating from Thailand, Vietnam and Laos, as well as Cambodia. The squid is tenderized with a little salt, sugar and lime juice and then grilled on skewers over hot coals or in a grill pan.

150 g/5 oz. dried cellophane noodles (see page 14–15)
500 g/1 lb. cleaned squid
½ teaspoon salt
½ teaspoon caster/ granulated sugar
1 tablespoon freshly squeezed lime juice
2 snake beans (see page 16), trimmed and very thinly sliced
1 long red chilli/chile, deseeded and thinly sliced
2 red Asian shallots (see page 16), thinly sliced
2 kaffir lime leaves (see page 156), very thinly sliced
1 lemon grass stalk, trimmed and very thinly sliced
a small handful each of fresh mint, coriander/cilantro and Thai basil leaves
Deep-fried shallots (see page 29), to serve

DRESSING
1 tablespoon freshly squeezed lime juice
1 teaspoon coriander/cilantro paste (see Tip)
2–3 teaspoons fish sauce
1–2 teaspoons caster/ granulated sugar

6–8 bamboo skewers, soaked in cold water for 30 minutes

Serves 4

Soak the noodles in a bowlful of hot water for 30 minutes until softened. Drain well with a clean kitchen cloth and set aside in a large mixing bowl.

To make the dressing, combine all the ingredients together in a small bowl and stir well to dissolve the sugar.

Next prepare the squid. Cut the cleaned squid bodies in half and score the inside of the flesh with a sharp knife to make a diamond pattern. Cut into 5-cm/2-in. pieces. Put the squid in a large mixing bowl and add the salt, sugar and lime juice, and rub well into the flesh. Set aside for 10 minutes and then thread the squid onto the pre-soaked skewers and set aside.

Meanwhile, put the remaining salad ingredients in a separate large mixing bowl, add 1 tablespoon of the dressing and toss well to coat. Add the noodles and toss again to mix.

Preheat a stovetop ridged grill pan over a high heat and when it starts to smoke cook the squid for 1 minute each side until charred. Remove the squid from the skewers and add to the noodles, drizzling the remaining dressing over the top. Toss well to coat and serve immediately, garnished with deep-fried shallots.

TIP: You can either make your own coriander/cilantro paste by pounding coriander/cilantro stalks, leaves and roots together in a pestle and mortar or, for ease, readymade sauces are available in the herb section of some larger supermarkets and work really well here.

Cucumber noodle salad with seared duck Laos

Traditionally, a cucumber salad is served simply as a side dish, but I like the combination of the shredded cucumber tossed with rice noodles alongside some seared duck for a lovely lunch dish.

250 g/9 oz. duck breast fillet
250 g/9 oz. dried rice vermicelli noodles (see page 14)
2 small cucumbers, deseeded
75 g/½ cup cherry tomatoes, quartered
2 red bird's eye chillies/chiles
1 garlic clove, roughly chopped
½ teaspoon salt
½ teaspoon caster/granulated sugar
freshly squeezed juice of ½ lime
2 teaspoons fish sauce
½ teaspoon shrimp paste (see page 21)

MARINADE
1 lemon grass stalk, trimmed and chopped

1 green chilli/chile, deseeded and chopped
2 garlic cloves, roughly chopped
a small bunch of fresh coriander/cilantro
2 tablespoons dark soy sauce
1 tablespoons fish sauce
2 teaspoons soft brown sugar

TO SERVE
toasted ground rice (see page 157)
chillies/chiles, sliced

Serves 4

Start by marinating the duck. Score the duck through the skin and into the flesh with a sharp knife and place in a shallow dish. Blend the marinade ingredients together in a food processor until smooth, then smother the duck, rubbing well into the scores. Cover and set in the fridge for 4 hours.

Soak the noodles in a bowlful of hot water for 20 minutes until softened. Drain well, pat dry with a kitchen cloth and set aside in a large mixing bowl.

Cut the cucumbers into batons and transfer to a large mixing bowl with the tomatoes. Put the chillies/chiles and garlic in a pestle and mortar with the salt and sugar and pound to form a paste. Stir in the lime juice, fish sauce and shrimp paste, then add to the cucumber mixture and stir well for several minutes until the cucumber is wilted.

Remove the duck from its marinade and cook on a preheated stovetop ridged grill pan (or heavy-based frying pan/skillet) for 4–5 minutes on each side. Remove from the pan and rest for 5 minutes before slicing.

Arrange the noodles on a plate and spoon the cucumber salad in the middle. Serve with the sliced, seared duck, garnished with toasted ground rice and red chillies/chiles.

Warm noodle and tofu salad Myanmar

This is a fascinating salad where several types of noodles – as well as rice, potato and tofu – are arranged in serving bowls with a whole range of toppings laid on the table for guests to help themselves. It's a fun way to put together just what you want. Use one or as many different types of noodle as you prefer.

200 g/7 oz. dried egg noodles, rice vermicelli, cellophane, or rice stick noodles (see pages 12–15)

100 g/½ cup plus 1 tablespoon basmati rice

1 teaspoon Chilli oil (see page 22)

100 g/4 oz. floury potatoes

100 g/2 cups deep-fried puffed tofu (see page 16)

125 g/about ¼ head iceberg/ butter lettuce, thinly sliced

100 g/2 cups silken/soft tofu (see page 157)

TOPPINGS

25 g/⅓ cup dried shrimp (see page 21)

25 g/⅓ cup chickpea/gram flour

1 quantity Crispy garlic and Garlic oil (see page 22)

1 quantity Baluchung (see page 29)

25 g/1½ tablespoons toasted ground rice (see page 157)

1 quantity Sweet and sour chilli sauce (see page 38)

2 limes, cut into wedges

a few fresh herbs, such as mint, coriander/cilantro and Thai basil

Serves 4

Start by preparing the toppings, as necessary. Take the dried shrimp and, using a pestle and mortar or spice grinder, pound to a 'floss'. Set aside. Toast the chickpea/gram flour in a dry frying pan/skillet set over a medium heat for 2–3 minutes. Set aside. Arrange everything in separate bowls on a tray in the middle of the table.

Prepare the noodles. Cook the egg noodles in a pan of boiling water for 3–4 minutes until al dente. Drain, rinse under cold water, drain again and dry thoroughly with a clean kitchen cloth. Soak the remaining noodles in a bowlful of hot water for 20–30 minutes until al dente. Drain well and dry thoroughly.

Cook the basmati rice according to packet instructions. Transfer to a bowl, stir in the chilli oil and set aside until cold.

Cook the potatoes in a pan of boiling water set over a medium heat for 10–12 minutes, until tender. Leave to cool completely before cutting into cubes. Set aside in a large mixing bowl.

To serve, spoon the noodles, rice, potatoes and deep-fried tofu into serving bowls and top each one with some shredded lettuce and silken/soft tofu. Then everyone can help themselves to the different toppings as wished.

stir-fries and curries

Stir-fries and curries

Stir-frying is a term we associate with Chinese and Asian cooking and is thought to be translated from the Chinese symbol 'chao', a technique similar to sautéing food in Western cultures. One of the things I like best about stir-fries is that they are one-pot meals, especially noodle stir-fries as all the ingredients are cooked together, making them the ideal fast food. Once all the elements are prepared the cooking time is minimal, as is the washing up afterwards!

In Asia, traditionally, food was always cooked on a fire rather than in an oven and hence stir-fries became an integral method of preparing and cooking food. The wok is thought to have originated in China as far back as 1300 AD although stir-frying as a cooking method developed slowly over many generations and wasn't part of everyday life in China until far later, perhaps well into the 18th and 19th centuries. Its popularity spread to Western cultures in the 19th and 20th centuries by early Asian migrants. Originally, in China, only the wealthy used woks for stir-fries as oil was expensive, but as it became cheaper its popularity grew. In the West, the spotlight on health and diet came into focus in the 1970s and because of this, the image of the wok as a healthy cooking medium exploded. The thought being was that only a little fat is required to cook a large quantity of vegetables and noodles with small amounts of meat or seafood.

Before I really discovered the secrets to successful stir-frying I have to admit I wasn't very good at it – I'd overcook the vegetables, add too much sauce or not enough sauce and end up with a sticky mass not nearly as delicious as those I'd eaten at restaurants or friends' homes. Then I got to work on a book by revered Chinese Australian chef Kylie Kwong. Billy Kwong was her Sydney restaurant originally set up as a shared business with Bill Granger. It was one of those restaurants where time stood still. What I mean is, ever since the day it opened in 2000 – to its recent closing – it retained its high standard of quite superb, modern Chinese cooking thanks to Kylie's hands-on approach, and the fact that it was her one and only restaurant in which she headed up the kitchen.

Watching Kylie and her head chef crafting beautiful dishes in vast woks over awesome heat in a tiny kitchen was an eye-opener and here are a few points I learned that have helped me improve and that I hope may well help you.

I can't stress the importance of a good quality wok.

Here's what you need to know about a wok and stir-frying. Go to Chinatown or your closest Chinese store and buy at carbon steel wok about 32 cm/13 in. across with a wooden handle. To season it, first wash it well in hot soapy water as it will be coated with oil from the factory, then rinse well. Set over a low heat for a couple of minutes until no water drops remain. You will then need a little vegetable oil, a couple of chopped spring onions/scallions and one sliced garlic clove. Set the wok over the highest heat setting you have for about 30 seconds. Remove from the heat and immediately add 2 tablespoons of the oil and swirl over the base and sides of the pan. Return the wok to a low heat, add the spring onions/scallions and garlic and stir-fry for about 15 minutes (yes it is quite a long time, but keep going, you only have to do this once), adding a little extra oil if needed. As you cook you will notice the wok turning colour from shiny steel to perhaps a little grey-blue through to yellow-brown. Once this is complete, remove from the heat and leave to cool for 10 minutes, before rinsing again (without soap). Finally return to a low heat and once more leave until no water drops remain. Remove from the heat and leave to cool. The wok is now seasoned and ready to use.

Secondly, always have a small bowl of cold water next to you as you cook. When you are stir-frying vegetables, after adding a few of the ingredients rather than continuing to add oil add a few splashes of water which will help steam the vegetables as they cook, allowing them to cook evenly. It also helps prevent the smaller ingredients such as garlic or ginger burning.

Thirdly, always prepare all your ingredients before you start to cook – this way you will manage to get everything cooked quickly without any of the ingredients over-cooking.

Finally, every time you finish cooking, immediately rinse the wok with water. Heat over a medium heat until completely dry and then brush a tiny bit of oil (using a clean kitchen cloth is best) over the base and sides of the wok.

You should now have a lovely seasoned wok and be equipped with a few helpful stir-frying tips.

Now you are all set, why not try out some of the more familiar noodle stir-fry dishes such as Prawn pad Thai (see page 146) and Singapore noodles (see page 133) or something a little less well known like the Prawn, crab and tamarind rice noodles (see page 145), where tamarind provides that sweet and sour flavour so important in South-east Asian dishes; or the Sweet potato noodles with broccoli in black bean sauce (see page 134). Here, Korean sweet potato noodles provide a lovely, chewy, substantial noodle perfect for the punchy black bean sauce.

As with all the chapters, I have tried to put together a selection of stir-fried noodle dishes that offer a good range of the different noodles with fish, meat and vegetarian options. I hope you find something delicious to cook and enjoy it as much as I have collecting and narrowing down my particular favourites.

Chinese American linguist Yeun Ren Chao (pure coincidence in his name) explains in a cookery book produced by his wife called *How to Cook and Eat in Chinese* published in 1945 that 'chao' (炒) technique could be translated as 'a big-fire-shallow-fat-continual-stirring-quick-frying of meat of cut-up material with wet seasoning. We shall call it "stir-fry" or "stir" for short.' Phew, thankfully we shortened it to stir-frying!

Szechuan beef noodles China

Szechuan is a province of China famous for its bold flavours, especially the pungent Szechuan peppercorn, which adds a delightful aromatic spiciness to dishes. Here it is used simply with beef strips and egg noodles.

300 g/1½ cups sliced beef fillet
2 tablespoons dark soy sauce
4 tablespoons sunflower oil
1 small onion, finely chopped
2 garlic cloves, crushed
2.5 cm/1 in. fresh ginger, grated
1 teaspoon Szechuan peppercorns (see page 19), toasted and ground
200 g/7 oz. dried egg noodles (see page 13)

SAUCE
200 ml/¾ cup hot Chicken stock (see page 25)
50 ml/scant ¼ cup shaoxing rice wine (see page 20)
2 tablespoons light soy sauce
2 tablespoons brown rice vinegar (see page 156)
1 tablespoon Asian sesame paste (see page 156)
2 teaspoons caster/granulated sugar

GARNISH
2 spring onions/scallions, trimmed and thinly sliced
a few sprigs of fresh coriander/cilantro

Serves 4

Start by making the sauce. Put all the ingredients in a bowl and stir well to dissolve the sesame paste. Set aside.

Put the sliced beef in a bowl with the soy sauce and set aside to marinate for at least 15 minutes.

Put 2 tablespoons of the oil in a wok set over a medium heat and stir-fry the marinated beef with its soy in batches for 3–4 minutes until browned. Remove the beef from the wok using a slotted spoon and set aside.

Add the remaining oil to the wok and fry the onion, garlic and ginger for 5 minutes. Stir in the sauce and peppercorns. Simmer for 5 minutes before returning the beef to the pan. Stir well and keep warm.

Meanwhile cook the noodles by plunging them into a large saucepan of boiling water. Return to the boil and cook for 2–3 minutes until al dente. Drain well and divide between warmed plates. Spoon the beef mixture over the top and garnish with spring onions/scallions and coriander/cilantro.

Serve at once.

Singapore noodles
China, Singapore and Malaysia

When on a stop-over in Singapore I often make a trip into the famous Glutton Bay area for a delicious bowl of noodles. To get the best dish check out the hawkers' stalls and go for the one with the longest queue.

2 teaspoons curry powder
300 g/2½ cups fresh egg noodles (see page 13)
2 tablespoons sunflower oil
300 g/4½ cups (about 30) prawns/shrimp, peeled and de-veined
75 g/3 oz. char sui (see page 156), sliced
a bunch of spring onions/scallions, trimmed and sliced
1 red (bell) pepper, deseeded and thinly sliced
2 eggs, beaten
2 tablespoons peanut oil
2 garlic cloves, sliced
2.5 cm/1 in. fresh ginger, peeled and cut into shreds
100 g/1¾ cups beansprouts, trimmed
6 garlic chives, snipped
garlic chive flowers (see page 19), to garnish
Sambal olek, to serve (see page 38)

SAUCE
2 tablespoons light soy sauce
1 tablespoon caster/granulated sugar
1 teaspoon sesame oil
2 tablespoons oyster sauce
2 tablespoons rice wine vinegar

Serves 4

Begin by making the sauce. Combine all the ingredients in a small mixing bowl and set aside.

Next combine the curry powder with 2 teaspoons water to make a paste. Set aside.

Cook the noodles by plunging them into a large saucepan of boiling water. Return to the boil and cook for 1 minute until al dente. Drain well and rinse under cold water to remove any excess starch. Set aside.

Put the sunflower oil in a wok or large frying pan/skillet set over a high heat and warm until smoking. Add the prawns/shrimp and stir-fry for 2–3 minutes until lightly golden. Remove with a slotted spoon and set aside.

Fry the char sui in the same pan for 1 minute, remove and set aside. Cook the spring onions/scallions and (bell) pepper for 2 minutes, remove from pan and set aside.

Reduce the heat, add the beaten egg and cook in a single layer for 2 minutes. Remove from the pan, roll up and allow to cool before cutting into thin strips.

Add the peanut oil to the wok and stir-fry the garlic and ginger for 1 minute, then stir in the reserved curry paste. Add the noodles to the pan with the reserved sauce and toss over a high heat for 2 minutes until heated through. Stir through the prawns/shrimp, char sui, spring onions/scallions, peppers, egg strips, beansprouts and chives for 1–2 minutes until hot.

Serve in bowls garnished with chive flowers and some sambal olek.

Sweet potato noodles with broccoli in black bean sauce Korea

Making your own black bean sauce rather than using ready-made gives a far lighter and, I think, better result, especially as it is so often served with vegetables. You can soak or wash the black beans if you like, but I prefer to cook them as they come, for added saltiness in the dish.

300 g/10 oz. sweet potato noodles (see page 15)
3 tablespoons peanut oil
5 cm/2 in. fresh ginger, peeled and thinly sliced
1 red onion, sliced
250 g/4 cups broccoli
sesame seeds, toasted, to garnish

BLACK BEAN SAUCE
2 tablespoons doenjang (see page 156)

125 ml/½ cup sake
60 ml/¼ cup mirin
2 tablespoons rice wine vinegar
2 tablespoons dark soy sauce
2 teaspoons sesame oil
3 tablespoons fermented black beans (see page 156)

Serves 4

Cook the noodles by plunging them into a large saucepan of boiling water. Return to the boil and cook for 1 minute until al dente. Drain well, refresh under cold water and shake dry. Set aside.

Next make the sauce. Whisk together the doenjang paste, sake, mirin, vinegar, soy sauce and sesame oil until smooth, then stir in the black beans. Set aside.

Heat the peanut oil in a wok or frying pan/skillet set over a medium heat and fry the ginger for 10 seconds until fragrant, add the onion and stir-fry for 1 minute, then stir in the broccoli and continue to stir-fry for 1 minute, adding 1 tablespoon cold water, until the broccoli is a vibrant green.

Add the sauce and cook for 2 minutes until the broccoli is tender. Finally add the noodles and stir until heated through.

Serve in bowls garnished with toasted sesame seeds.

Grilled beef skewers with yakisoba noodles *Japan*

This is the Japanese version of the familiar and popular Chinese dish chow mein and is traditionally made with buckwheat noodles although it is common to use any type of wheat noodle. You can buy yakisoba noodles and yakisoba sauce but I prefer to make my own sauce and use whatever noodles I have to hand.

350 g/13 oz. beef fillet
2 tablespoons dark soy sauce
1 tablespoon mirin
1 tablespoon sake
1 teaspoon sesame oil
200 g/7 oz. dried yakisoba or egg thread noodles (see page 12–13)
2 tablespoons vegetable oil
1 small red onion, thinly sliced
1 small carrot, cut into batons
1 small courgette/zucchini, cut into batons
125 g/2 cups sliced white cabbage
2 spring onions/scallions, trimmed and thinly sliced

YAKISOBA SAUCE
2 tablespoons oyster sauce
2 tablespoons tonkatsu sauce (see Tip)
1 teaspoon salt
1 teaspoon caster/granulated sugar

GARNISHES
1 tablespoon powdered seaweed (see page 157)
Pickled cucumbers (see page 30), shredded
dried bonito flakes (see page 21, optional)

8 metal skewers

Serves 4

Cut the beef into thin slices and put in a bowl. Add the soy sauce, mirin, sake and sesame oil, and set aside to marinate for 1 hour. Strain, reserving the marinade, and thread the beef slices onto metal skewers.

Meanwhile, cook the noodles by plunging them into a large saucepan of boiling water. Return to the boil and cook for 3–4 minutes until al dente. Drain, refresh under cold water, drain again and shake dry. Set aside.

Whisk all the sauce ingredients together in a small mixing bowl and stir in the reserved beef marinade.

Preheat the oven to 110°C (225°F) Gas ¼ (or the lowest heat setting).

Preheat a stovetop ridged grill pan or heavy frying pan/skillet over a high heat and sear the beef skewers on all sides for 2 minutes until charred and tender. Transfer the skewers to a baking sheet, turn off the oven and set in the still-warm oven while you cook the remaining beef in the same way.

Meanwhile, heat the vegetable oil in a wok or large frying pan/skillet and stir-fry the onion and carrot for 2 minutes, then add the courgette/zucchini and cabbage and stir-fry for 1 minute. Add the noodles, spring onions/scallions and sauce and stir-fry for a further 2 minutes until the noodles are heated through.

Arrange the noodles on plates with the beef skewers and serve topped with the garnishes.

TIP: Tonkatsu sauce is a Japanese condiment similar in flavour to Worcestershire sauce but thicker in consistency. It is readily available from Japanese and Asian food stores.

Hokkein noodles Singapore

The name 'Hokkein noodles' refers both to a type of noodle and a noodle dish. Originally from the Hokkein province in China, the noodles and the dish spread in popularity to Malaysia and Singapore, and today are synonymous with stir-fried noodles around the world. An authentic Singaporean Hokkein mee is made with prawns/shrimp rather than pork, but this was cooked for me by a friend who spent several years in Singapore, and it was delicious.

2 teaspoons freshly grated ginger
3 tablespoons shaoxing rice wine (see page 20)
3 tablespoons light soy sauce
2 teaspoons sesame oil
300 g/1½ cups sliced pork fillet
500 g/4 cups fresh Hokkein noodles (or 250 g/9 oz. dried, see page 13)
4 tablespoons peanut oil
2 carrots, sliced
1 red (bell) pepper, deseeded and sliced
4 garlic cloves, sliced
150 g/2½ cups shiitake mushrooms (see page 16), thinly sliced
2 tablespoons oyster sauce
2 tablespoons ketjap manis (see page 156)
4 spring onions/scallions, trimmed and sliced, plus extra, thinly sliced to garnish

Serves 4

Whisk together the ginger, shaoxing, soy sauce and sesame oil in a shallow dish. Add the pork slices, toss well and set aside to marinate for 30 minutes. Remove the pork from the marinade and reserve both.

Meanwhile cook the noodles by plunging them into a large saucepan of boiling water. Return to the boil and cook for 1–2 minutes until al dente. Drain, immediately refresh under cold water, drain again and dry well with a clean kitchen cloth. Set aside.

Put 2 tablespoons of the peanut oil in a wok and set over a medium heat until it starts to shimmer. Add the marinated pork and stir-fry for 2–3 minutes until lightly golden. Remove with a slotted spoon and set aside.

Heat the remaining oil in the wok and fry the carrots for 1 minute, add the (bell) pepper and garlic and fry for a further minute. Then stir in the mushrooms and fry for a further 2 minutes. Add the noodles and stir-fry for 1 minute.

Add the cooked pork, reserved marinade, oyster sauce, ketjap manis, 25 ml/ scant 2 tablespoons water and spring onions/scallions, and stir-fry until the noodles are hot.

Divide between bowls and serve garnished with spring onions/scallions.

Crab and noodle stir-fry Malaysia

This Malay version of Singapore crab was served to me on a trip to a small island, rather unattractively named Mud Island. However, where there's mud there are mud crabs and this tiny island built on stilts, just off the west coast of Malaysia, is home to thousands of crabs and almost as many restaurants serving delicious platefuls of crab any which way. This was my choice and it was awesome.

1 onion, roughly chopped

4 garlic cloves

2.5 cm/1 in. fresh ginger, peeled and chopped

2 small red bird's eye chillies/chiles

1 tablespoon shrimp paste (see page 21)

3 tablespoons peanut oil

50 ml/scant ¼ cup shoaxing rice wine (see page 20)

250 ml/1 cup tomato passata

250 ml/1 cup Chicken stock (see page 25)

3 tablespoons light soy sauce

1 tablespoons ketjap manis (see page 156)

1 kg/2 lbs. fresh crab, prepared (see Tip)

2 spring onions/scallions, trimmed and finely chopped

400 g/generous 3 cups fresh egg noodles (or 200 g/7 oz. dried egg noodles, see page 13)

spring onions/scallions, thinly sliced, to garnish

Serves 4

Put the onion, garlic, ginger and chillies/chiles in a food processor and blend to a smooth paste. Stir in the shrimp paste and set aside for a moment.

Heat the oil in a wok or large frying pan/skillet set over a medium heat and fry the paste for 3–4 minutes until fragrant. Add the shaoxing and simmer for 1 minute before stirring in the passata, stock, soy sauce and ketjap manis. Cook for 10 minutes until thickened.

Add the prepared crab and spring onions/scallions, stir well, cover and simmer for 5–8 minutes until the crab is cooked through.

Meanwhile, cook the noodles by plunging them into a large saucepan of boiling water. Return to the boil and cook for 4 minutes until al dente. Drain the noodles, shake well to remove excess water and divide between serving dishes.

Spoon the crab sauce over the top of each dish and serve sprinkled with extra spring onions/scallions.

TIP: It's best to use a live crab for this recipe, so ask your fishmonger to kill the crab for you and, if possible, to cut it up ready to stir-fry. Alternatively, view the process online to see how to do it yourself. If you don't feel confident doing this, use 1 kg/2 lbs. cooked crab claws, cracking the shells with a hammer and continue as above.

Flat noodle stir-fry with prawn and Chinese sausage Malaysia

This Malay version of Pad Thai combines both Thai and Chinese elements and goes some way to portraying the blend of culinary cultures so typical of the country. This recipe serves two but can easily be doubled to serve up to four people.

100 g/3½ oz. dried rice stick noodles (see page 14)
1½ tablespoons vegetable oil
2 garlic cloves, crushed
2 Asian shallots (see page 16), thinly sliced
12 prawns/shrimp, peeled and de-veined
1 Chinese dried sausage (see page 156), sliced
75 g/1⅓ cups beansprouts, trimmed
200 g/7 oz. fish cake, sliced
1 egg
1 tablespoon Sambal olek (see page 38)
1 tablespoon chopped garlic chives

SAUCE
2 tablespoons light soy sauce
1 tablespoon fish sauce
1 teaspoon caster/granulated sugar
¼ teaspoon ground white pepper

TO SERVE
spring onions/scallions, thinly sliced
a bunch of fresh coriander/cilantro
garlic chive flowers (see page 19)

Serves 2

Soak the noodles in a bowlful of hot water for 20–30 minutes until softened. Drain well, pat dry with a clean kitchen cloth and set aside in a mixing bowl.

To make the sauce, whisk all the ingredients together in a small mixing bowl. Set aside.

Heat the oil in a large wok or large frying pan/skillet set over a medium–high heat and add the garlic and shallots, frying for 20 seconds. Add the prawns/shrimp and sliced sausage and stir-fry for 2 minutes until the prawns/shrimp change colour. Then add the beansprouts and sliced fish cake and stir-fry for 1 minute.

Stir in the noodles and sauce, and with a spatula push the noodles to one side to make a hole. Crack the egg into the middle and break the yolk to blend with the white. Spoon the noodles back over the egg and leave for about 15 seconds.

Add the sambal olek and garlic chives and continue to stir-fry until the egg is cooked and the chives start to wilt.

Spoon into bowls and serve garnished with spring onions/scallions, coriander/cilantro and garlic chive flowers.

Prawn, crab and tamarind rice noodles Vietnam

Tamarind is one of the ingredients used in South-east Asia to impart the sour flavour that the cuisine is renowned for. Here, paired with the prawns/shrimp, asparagus and crab, it is quite delightful.

200 g/7 oz. cellophane noodles (see page 14)
2 tablespoons peanut oil
4 garlic cloves, sliced
1 red onion, sliced
½ tablespoon freshly ground black pepper
350 g/4¼ cups (about 35) prawns/shrimp, shelled, de-veined and butterflied
350 g/3 cups asparagus tips, trimmed and cut into 5-cm/2-in. pieces
250 g/½ cup picked fresh crab meat
2 spring onions/scallions, trimmed and sliced
4 tablespoons chopped fresh coriander/cilantro, plus extra to serve

TAMARIND SAUCE
125 ml/½ cup tamarind water (see page 21)
2 tablespoons fish sauce
2 tablespoons grated palm sugar (see page 21)

Serves 4

Soak the noodles in a bowlful of hot water for 10–20 minutes until softened. Drain well, shake dry and set aside in a large mixing bowl.

To make the sauce, whisk all the ingredients together in a small mixing bowl, stirring well to dissolve the sugar. Set aside.

Heat the oil in a wok or large frying pan/skillet set over a medium–high heat. Add the garlic, stir-fry for 10 seconds and then add the onion and pepper. Stir-fry for 2 minutes, then add the prawns/shrimp and asparagus and continue to stir-fry for 2 minutes until the prawns/shrimp are cooked through.

Add the crab meat and tamarind sauce and cook for 2 minutes. Add the noodles, spring onions/scallions and coriander/cilantro, stir-fry until the noodles are heated through and serve immediately with extra coriander/cilantro sprinkled on top.

Prawn pad Thai Thailand

Probably the best known of all Thai dishes, pad Thai in its simplest form is a basic combination of fried noodles with tofu, egg and bean sprouts. Fresh cooked prawns/shrimp add a touch of luxury to the dish.

Soak noodles in warm water for 30 minutes or until soft. Drain well.

In the meantime, make the sauce. In a small saucepan, heat the palm sugar, white sugar, tamarind water, fish sauce, soy sauce and 2 tablespoons of cold water, stirring for 2 minutes, to dissolve the sugar. Set aside.

Heat half the oil in a wok over a medium heat until it starts to shimmer. Add the garlic and spring onions/scallions, and stir-fry for 30 seconds. Remove from the pan with a slotted spoon and set aside. Then add the prawns/shrimp to the pan and stir-fry for 3 minutes. Remove from the pan and set aside. Finally, add the tofu to the pan and stir-fry for 3–4 minutes or until crispy. Pour in the beaten egg and cook, stirring until it sets around the tofu. Remove the tofu and egg mix with a slotted spoon to a small bowl and carefully break it up. Set aside.

Add the remaining oil to the pan and fry the soaked dried prawns/shrimp for 30 seconds, then add the drained noodles, stir-fried prawns/shrimp, garlic, onions and tofu and egg mixture to the pan. Stir well and then pour in the sauce. Cook, stirring for 1 minute or until everything is nicely heated through. Finally, add most of the bean sprouts (reserving some to serve) and coriander/cilantro and cook for 30 seconds, until the leaves have wilted.

Pile onto plates and top with the reserved bean sprouts, crushed peanuts, coriander/cilantro leaves and a sprinkling of cayenne pepper. Serve with lime wedges.

125 g/4½ oz. dried flat rice noodles (see page 15)
3 tablespoons vegetable oil
2 garlic cloves, thickly sliced
2 spring onions/scallions, trimmed and sliced into 2.5-cm/1-inch lengths
12 medium raw prawns/shrimp, peeled and de-veined
100 g/scant 1 cup tofu, diced
1 egg, lightly beaten
2 teaspoons dried prawns/shrimp, (see page 21)
50 g/1 cup bean sprouts
2 tablespoons coriander/cilantro leaves

SAUCE
2-cm/¾-inch cube palm sugar, finely grated (see page 21)
1½ tablespoons white sugar
1½ tablespoons tamarind water
2 tablespoons fish sauce
2 teaspoons light soy sauce

TO SERVE
2 tablespoons peanuts, crushed
coriander/cilantro leaves
a pinch of cayenne pepper
1 lime, cut into wedges

Serves 2

Squid with chillies and holy basil Thailand

One of my favourite Thai stir-fries, I love the simplicity of this dish. Chillies/chiles and Thai basil leaves are the predominate flavours whilst the sauce has a delightful sweetness to it.

250 g/7 oz. dried egg thread noodles
  (see page 13)
2 dried red chillies/chiles
1 large red chilli/chile, deseeded and
  chopped
1–2 tablespoons peanut oil
2 garlic cloves, crushed
400 g/13 oz. cleaned squid bodies
150 g/a large handful sugar snap peas,
  trimmed and cut in half lengthways

a small bunch of fresh Thai basil

SAUCE
3 tablespoons Chicken stock (see
  page 25)
2 tablespoons fish sauce
2 tablespoons light soy sauce
2 tablespoons caster/granulated sugar

Serves 4

Cook the noodles by plunging them into a large saucepan of boiling water. Return to the boil and cook for 4 minutes until al dente. Drain well, refresh under cold water and shake dry. Set aside.

To make the sauce, pour the stock, fish sauce and soy sauce into a small mixing bowl. Stir in the sugar to dissolve and set aside.

Put the dried chillies/chiles in a bowl and pour over boiling water to cover. Leave to soak for 15 minutes until softened, remove from the water and finely chop.

Heat the oil in a wok set over a medium heat until it starts to shimmer. Add the garlic, soaked and fresh chillies/chiles, and stir-fry for 10 seconds until fragrant. Immediately add the squid and stir-fry for 30 seconds. Add the sugar snap peas and stir-fry for 1 minute.

Add the noodles and sauce and stir-fry for a further minute, until the squid is cooked and tender.

Add the Thai basil, toss well and serve at once.

2 red Asian shallots (see
    page 16), chopped
1 garlic clove, roughly chopped
1 cm/½ in. fresh turmeric
    (or ½ teaspoon ground)
a pinch of salt
1 tablespoon Thai red curry
    paste
100 ml/⅓ cup coconut cream
2 tablespoons grated palm
    sugar (see pages 20–21)
1 tablespoon fish sauce
2 teaspoons dark soy sauce
600 ml/2½ cups Chicken stock
    (see page 25)
4 kaffir lime leaves (see
    page 156), pounded
250 g/1 cup thinly sliced beef
    fillet
2 tablespoons chopped fresh
    coriander/cilantro
500 g/1 lb./4 cups fresh egg
    noodles
vegetable oil, for deep frying

TO SERVE
spring onions/scallions
Deep-fried shallots
    (see page 29)
1 lime, cut into wedges

Serves 4

Chiang Mai noodle curry Thailand

As the name suggests, this dish originates from Chiang Mai
in the north of Thailand. It can be served as a soup or a stew-
like dish of noodles with a curried coconut sauce.

Put the shallots, garlic, turmeric and salt in a pestle and mortar and pound
until fairly smooth. Stir in the red curry paste.

Add the coconut cream to a wok set over a medium heat and cook for about
3 minutes until the cream bubbles and splits. Stir in curry paste mixture and
continue to cook for a further 2 minutes. Stir in the palm sugar, fish sauce and
soy sauce, and bring to the boil. Add the chicken stock and lime leaves and
simmer gently for 15 minutes.

Meanwhile, pour vegetable oil into a wok or large saucepan to reach about
5 cm/2 in. up the side of the pan and set over a medium heat. Test the
temperature of the pan by dropping a cube of bread into the hot oil – it should
crisp within 30 seconds. Carefully add 50 g/2 oz./⅓ cup of the noodles and
deep-fry (be careful as the oil will spit) until crisp. Drain on paper towels and
set aside to garnish.

Cook the remaining noodles by plunging them into a large saucepan of boiling
water. Return to the boil and cook for 2–3 minutes until al dente. Drain well
and divide between warmed bowls.

Stir the beef and coriander/cilantro into the wok with the curry mixture and
immediately remove the pan from the heat.

Spoon the curried beef and sauce over the noodles and serve with the
deep-fried noodles, spring onions/scallions, deep-fried shallots
and lime wedges.

Stir-fried fish and ginger noodles Cambodia

This is such a simple yet delicious dish, which I often serve with a side of simple stir-fried Asian greens. Traditionally, in Cambodia, the ginger would be far younger and fresher than the varieties we find in Europe, but it still works really well.

400 g/14 oz. fish fillets,
  such as snapper or bream
1 tablespoon light soy sauce
3 tablespoons rice flour
2 tablespoons fish sauce
1 tablespoon caster/
  granulated sugar
1 teaspoon shrimp paste (see
  page 21)
freshly squeezed juice of 1 lime
8 tablespoons vegetable oil
5 cm/2 in. fresh ginger, peeled
  and thinly sliced
2 garlic cloves, sliced
1 large red chilli/chile,
  deseeded and chopped
50 g/⅓ cup mangetout/snow
  peas, thinly sliced
a bunch of spring
  onions/scallions
200 g/7 oz. dried egg thread
  noodles (see page 14)

Serves 4

Remove any small bones from the fish using fish tweezers and cut the fillets into 3.5-cm/1½-in. pieces. Put in a shallow dish and pour over the soy sauce. Set aside to marinate for 30 minutes.

Remove the fish pieces from the marinade, reserving any leftover soy sauce, and dust with the rice flour. Set aside.

Whisk the fish sauce, sugar, shrimp paste, lime juice and any remaining marinade together in a bowl, stirring until the sugar is dissolved.

Heat all but 2 tablespoons of the oil in a wok or large frying pan/skillet set over a medium heat. Add the fish pieces and cook for 2–3 minutes, turning on all sides, until crispy. Remove from the pan and drain on paper towels. Discard the oil, wipe the pan clean and return to the heat with the remaining 2 tablespoons of oil.

Add the ginger, garlic and chilli/chile, and fry for 1 minute until fragrant. Add the mangetout/snow peas and spring onions/scallions, stir well, then add the sauce and 2 tablespoons water. Simmer for 1 minute, then stir in the fish pieces and warm through for 2–3 minutes.

Meanwhile plunge the noodles into a large saucepan of boiling water. Return to the boil and cook for 2–3 minutes until al dente. Drain well and transfer to a serving platter.

Arrange the fish and sauce on top and serve at once.

Crispy noodles with stir-fried greens   Laos

To the north of Laos lies the Yunnan region of China and many dishes have migrated over the border into Laos. Here Chinese egg noodles are used rather than the rice noodles that are more typical of Laotian dishes. Use any green leaves you like for this dish – anything goes.

200 g/7 oz. dried egg thread
  noodles (see page 13)
4 tablespoons vegetable oil
1 tablespoon soy sauce
2 garlic cloves, sliced
4 spring onions/scallions,
  trimmed and thickly sliced
500 g/9 cups mixed greens,
  choose from pak choi/bok
  choy, choi sum (see page
  16), spinach or kale
a handful each of fresh basil
  and coriander/cilantro
1 tablespoon sesame seeds,
  toasted

SAUCE
2 tablespoons oyster sauce
1 tablespoon fermented soy
  bean paste (see page 156)
1 tablespoon dark soy sauce
2 teaspoons sesame oil
1 teaspoon grated palm sugar
  (see page 21)

Serves 4

Cook the noodles by plunging them into a large saucepan of boiling water. Return to the boil and cook for 5 minutes, until al dente. Drain well, refresh under cold water and shake dry. Set aside.

Stir all the sauce ingredients together in a small mixing bowl, adding 3 tablespoons cold water, and set aside.

Preheat half the vegetable oil in a wok set over a medium heat and add the noodles in one layer. Add the soy sauce and fry for 2–3 minutes until starting to brown, then flip over and cook for a further 2–3 minutes until crispy. Remove the noodles from the pan and transfer to a warmed platter.

Add the remaining oil to the wok and fry the garlic and spring onions/scallions for 1 minute until wilted. Add the mixed greens and stir-fry for 1–2 minutes until wilted. Stir in the sauce and cook for 1 minute.

Spoon the vegetables and sauce over the noodles and top with the herbs and sesame seeds. Serve at once.

Glossary

ASIAN PEAR

Also called 'nashi' pear, this fruit looks more like an apple but is in fact an Asian pear variety. They have a crisp, juicy flesh and are great in salads.

ASIAN SESAME PASTE

This differs slightly from the Middle Eastern sesame paste as it is made from unhulled sesame seeds, which give it a slightly more bitter flavour.

BANANA STEM

Considered a vegetable in Thai cooking, the stem is actually tightly rolled up banana leaves. The edible centre is both soft and nutritious.

BLACK CLOUD EAR FUNGUS

Also called 'cloud ear', 'wood' or 'mousse ear' fungus, this mushroom is usually sold dried. Valued for its delightful crisp texture, especially in Chinese cooking.

BROWN RICE VINEGAR

This is the same as clear rice wine vinegar but made from brown rice, as the name suggests. Either could be used in the recipes within this book.

CHAR SUI

This barbecued pork is named after a literal translation of 'fork-roast', describing the cooking method where long strips of pork are skewered onto forks and cooked over a barbecue. It has a delicious smoky, slightly sweet flavour and is often served in noodle soups.

CHICKPEA/GRAM FLOUR

This flour made from ground chickpeas is used in both Indian and Asian cookery. A distinctive pale yellow colour with a slight nutty flavour, it is gluten-free.

CHINESE BLACK VINEGAR

From the Zhenjiang province of China, this dark-coloured vinegar (sometimes called 'Chinkiang' vinegar) is made from a mixture of glutinous rice and malt. It has a deep, malty flavour not dissimilar to balsamic vinegar.

CHINESE CABBAGE

There is no Chinese word for cabbage but the type used in this book is normally referred to as Chinese cabbage in Europe (or 'Napa cabbage' in the US). It is a light green elongated salad vegetable with crinkly leaves.

CHINESE DRIED SAUSAGE

A generic term for a whole variety of dried sausages used in Chinese cooking. Look out for Lap Cheong, a pork sausage that is smoked, sweetened and seasoned with rice wine and soy sauce.

CHINESE FIVE-SPICE POWDER

This mix of spices includes star anise, cloves, Chinese cinnamon, Szechuan pepper and fennel.

DOENJANG

A Korean bean paste made from dried soy beans, it is often served as an accompaniment to vegetables as a dipping sauce but is also used to thicken other sauces. Available from Asian food stores.

DRIED KOREAN CHILLI FLAKES

Also known as 'gochugaru', these coarsely ground chilli/chile flakes are unique to Korea and have a sweet, spicy flavour that builds as you eat them but doesn't overwhelm the palate. Available from Asian supermarkets or online.

FERMENTED BLACK BEANS

Of Chinese origin, these are black soya beans that are fermented and then preserved by salting. They are sold either canned or in a vacuum pack and can be rinsed before using, but taste first and rinse only if necessary.

FERMENTED SOY BEAN PASTE

A spicy, salty paste made largely from soy beans, indigenous to East and Far East Asia, where they are used as a condiment to flavour dishes such as stir-fries.

GOCHUJANG

A fiery Korean chilli/chile paste with a deep red colour made from red chillies, glutinous rice, fermented soy beans and salt.

KAFFIR LIME LEAVES

The leaves of the kaffir lime tree, also known as 'makrut lime' and native to South-east Asia, has exceptionally fragrant leaves that are shredded into salads, stir-fires and soups.

KETJAP MANIS

A sweetened soy sauce from Indonesia where it is known as 'kecap manis' – 'kecap' is a generic term for fermented sauces and probably takes its name from the English 'ketchup'.

LOTUS ROOT

The symbol of purity in Buddhism, this is the edible root of the lotus flower. The roots are rhizomes, pinkish red in colour with thin tunnels running through the length of the root. Cut into thin slices, it can be deep-fried or cooked in soups.

MARINATED TOFU

This is regular tofu that is sold pre-marinated in various sauces and flavourings. Those who find plain tofu a bit bland should try this out. It is delicious in salads.

MICRO HERBS

These seem to be one of those ingredients that has come to our attention and its popularity has snowballed – partly due to their cuteness but largely because they are nutritionally power-packed little leaves that add a wonderful punch of flavour to salads and other dishes. Easy to grow, they are early harvested seedlings and can be anything from basil, fennel and radish to Asian plants such as perilla, mustard greens and shiso. They are available from some greengrocers, larger supermarkets or online.

MIRIN

A sweet rice wine from Japan, Mirin is often used to balance the savoury flavours in noodle soups, marinades and dressings.

NORI

A type of dried seaweed best known for its role in making sushi, it is also used as a garnish on many Japanese dishes, especially soba noodles.

PICKLED GARLIC

Pickles are a popular condiment in Asian cooking and garlic is no exception. Available in jars from Asian stores, once opened it keeps well in the fridge for up to 1 month.

POTATO FLOUR

The starch extracted from potatoes is often used as a thickening ingredient. It is also used alongside rice flour in Asian dishes. Rice flour can be substituted.

POWDERED SEAWEED

Often made from kombu and edible kelp, seaweed powder is sold commercially in Japan as a seasoning ingredient for rice and noodle dishes.

RICE FLOUR

The starch extracted from rice is used as a thickening agent in Asian dishes, as well as being used to make rice noodles and wrappers.

SAKE

The Japanese equivalent to white wine when used in cooking, sake is made from fermented rice, as is soju, the Korean equivalent.

SEVEN-SPICE POWDER

This mix of spices includes chilli/hot red pepper powder, dried orange peel, black and white sesame seeds, Szechuan peppercorns, ground ginger and dried seaweed.

SILKEN/SOFT TOFU

Is a softer, paler tofu from Japan where it is known as 'kinugoshi'. It has a finer consistency than other types of tofu. Perhaps best known for its use in miso soup, silken/soft tofu is also lovely in salads.

SPRING ROLL WRAPPERS

Not to be confused with either gyoza wrappers or wonton wrappers, these are used specifically for making spring rolls. Sold in square or round sheets, the texture is like a very fine, almost lacy pancake.

TOASTED GROUND RICE

Used mainly in Thai cookery, toasted ground rice is made by toasting grains of rice in a wok and then grinding them in a pestle and mortar to form a powder. It is traditionally used in large salads and has a smokey, nutty flavour.

WASABI PASTE

Wasabi paste is traditionally used in making sushi as well as a condiment served alongside sushi and sashimi. Due to its fiery nature the root is known as 'Japanese horseradish', although it is not part of the horseradish family.

WASABI POWDER

Originally, this Japanese condiment was made from the wasabi root, although today it is more commonly made from a combination of wasabi, English horseradish, mustard greens and even spirulina, which is used as a colouring agent. If you can, buy pure wasabi powder for its superior eye-watering flavour and add a little water to make a paste.

WONTON WRAPPERS

Made from wheat flour and eggs, wonton wrappers are used to make Chinese dumplings.

YELLOW BEAN SAUCE

Used primarily in Beijing cuisine and other regions in northern China as a condiment in sauces. Despite the fact it is made from yellow soy beans, salt and water, it is actually a deep mustardy brown colour.

Index

Acknowledgments

While researching and writing this cookbook I found myself constantly revisiting not only places, but friends, acquaintances and chefs who have kindly shared their food with me over the past 20 years or so, and opened my eyes and tummy to some of the best dishes on the planet. Of these I would like to thank Kylie Kwong and Martin Boetz who ran two of Sydney's best Asian restaurants and whose skill in preparing the most exquisite food is unquestionable. Thank you to friends Theressa Klein for her knowledge of Singapore and Thai cooking and Melanie Szeto for sharing many yum cha meals with me and ordering dishes I would never have tried. Thank you to Hugh Ngyuen who introduced me to the amazing world of Vietnamese cuisine and has taught me many skills along the way.

Thank you to everyone from Ryland Peters & Small who have made the whole process seamless, fun and I am sure fruitful. Sonya Nathoo you were a delight to work with and I look forward to learning more about Indian food from you. Julia Charles you continue to put your faith in me and I am forever grateful. I would like to thank Leslie Harrington for agreeing to let me shoot this book with my husband Ian Wallace, whose skill in producing beautiful food images makes me smile constantly and of whom I am very proud.

A very special thanks goes to stylist Tony Hutchinson, who had the unfavourable job of getting between a husband and wife team who are very fussy and used to always getting their own way. Your styling has made this book very special and where would we have been with out all those Hobnobs! Thank you to Daniella Sanchez for always having a smile on your face and who was a joy to have helping me in the kitchen.

Lastly, although I have already mentioned you, Ian thank you, not only for taking lovely pictures but you put up with me and that's a skill in itself.